BALANCED MEASURES
FOR
STRATEGIC PLANNING
A Public Sector Handbook

BALANCED MEASURES
FOR
STRATEGIC PLANNING
A Public Sector Handbook

Kathleen E. Monahan

MANAGEMENTCONCEPTS

Vienna, Virginia

***

MANAGEMENTCONCEPTS

8230 Leesburg Pike, Suite 800
Vienna, Virginia 22182
Phone: (703) 790-9595
Fax: (703) 790-1371
Web: www.managementconcepts.com

Printed in the United States of America

Library of Congress Cataloging-in-Publication Data

Monahan, Kathleen, E., 1946–
   Balanced measures for strategic planning : a public sector handbook /
   Kathleen E. Monahan.
      p.   cm.
   Includes bibliographical references and index.
   IBSN 1-56726-096-9 (hc.)
   1. Total quality management in government. 2. Benchmarking
   (Management)   3. Performance technology. 4. Public administration.
   5. Strategic planning. I. Title.

JF1525.T67 M65   2000
352.3'4—dc21

                                                        00-046291

About the Author

Kathleen E. Monahan served as project director for the Best Practices Report of Balanced Measures for NPR. She has been with the federal government for 17 years and has worked with GPRA-related issues since enactment of the legislation in 1993. Kathy is currently an analyst in the Division of Policy and Planning in the Immigration and Naturalization Service, U.S. Department of Justice. She was formerly with the Office of the CFO at the Department of Housing and Urban Development. She has a double Master's Degree in Foreign Languages and Education from West Virginia University.

Table of Contents

Preface xi

Chapter 1. Introduction to Using a Balanced Approach
in the Public Sector 1
History of Strategic Planning in the Public Sector 1
History of the Balanced Approach 6
Application of a Balanced Approach to the
    Public Sector 10
Why a Balanced Approach Works 18

Chapter 2. Determining Public Value: Meeting Public
Governance and Client Responsibilities 21
The Difference Between a Customer and a Stakeholder 25
The Value Chain 25
The Consultation Process 28
Identifying Your Customer and Stakeholder 30
Why Regulatory and Enforcement Agencies Are
    (and Are *Not*) Different 32
Case Study #1: State of Iowa 34
Case Study #2: Bureau of Land Management 38
Case Study #3: City of Coral Springs, Florida 43
Case Study #4: Natural Resources of Canada 47

Chapter 3. Organizing Your Consultation: Assessing
Current Reality and Planning for the Future 53
The Strategic Planning Process 53
Formulating the Mission Statement 60
Focus Groups 62
Workshops/Retreats 67
Brainstorming 68
SWOT Assessments 69
A Word about Putting It All Together 72

Case Study #1: U.S. Postal Service............................ 73
Case Study #2: State of Texas 79
Case Study #3: City of Phoenix, Arizona 82

**Chapter 4. Consultation at Its Best: Involving Everyone
in the Process** 87
Listening to Your Customers and Stakeholders 88
Consulting with Legislative Bodies......................... 90
Listening to Your Employees 91
Partnering with Unions 95
Case Study #1: Social Security Administration............... 96
Case Study #2: City of Austin, Texas 102
Case Study #3: County of Fairfax, Virginia 104

Chapter 5. The Need to Communicate 109
Developing a Communications Strategy 110
Changing the Management Style through
    Communication 110
Performance by the Organization, Teams, and
    the Individual 116
Town Halls and Other Meeting Alternatives 118
Communicating Internally and Externally, and Where to
    Differentiate... 120
The Need for Honesty in Establishing Public Trust 121
Case Study #1: Internal Revenue Service 122
Case Study #2: City of Charlotte, North Carolina 135
Case Study #3: Commonwealth of Virginia 140

**Chapter 6. Leading the Public Sector Organization
in a Changing World** 143
Sharing the Leadership Role 146
The Leader as Educator 148
The Leader as Architect................................. 149
The Leader as Caretaker 150
Establishing Strong Performance Management
    Principles 151
Case Study #1: Veterans Benefits Administration 154
Case Study #2: St. Lawrence Seaway Management
    Corporation 160
Case Study #3: Florida Department of Environmental
    Protection 166

**Chapter 7: Making It All Work: Building a Strategic
Framework** 175
Linking Your Plan to Day-to-Day Operations 176
Linking Your Plan to the Business Plan 178
Linking Your Plan to the Data Systems 179
Linking Your Plan to the Budget Process 180
Creating a Strategic Management Framework 182
Case Study #1: United States Coast Guard 191
Case Study #2: Department of Housing and Urban
Development 199

A Final Word 203

Notes 207

Appendix 209

Index 225

Preface

This book is an outgrowth of a study done for the National Partnership for Reinventing Government (NPR). It does not purport to be a textbook on the subject, but rather a reference book of ideas for those involved in the day-to-day struggle with performance management and measurement.

With the author serving as the project leader for the NPR study, a core team was formed in February 1999 that included representatives from both federal organizations and state and local governments. Leaders were selected from among the core team members to head up the study's three cluster teams: the High Impact Agency Team, the State and Local Government Team, and the Regulatory Agencies Team. These teams represented the division of responsibility for public sector organizations that the core team wanted to review for best practices. The core team also agreed to look at the experiences of foreign governments, such as the United Kingdom and Canada.

The cluster leaders formed their respective teams, each of which included individuals from many of the resource partners listed in the study. The team leaders briefed the core team on cluster activities at weekly meetings.

The NPR study was not a formal benchmarking study; rather, its purpose was to seek out the best practices and lessons learned by public and private sector entities in their performance planning and management. However, while the methodology did not include all the elements of a benchmarking study, the team adopted the Benchmarking Code of Conduct (published by the American Productivity & Quality Center) because it incorporates principles applicable to the study.

The Balanced Measures Study Team investigated and reported on answers to the following questions: How do leading organizations balance their performance measurement among business results, customer service, and employee satisfaction? More specifically, how do they use their customers, stakeholders, and employees to establish and prioritize performance measures in the strategic planning process? How do successful organizations achieve management and employee "buy-in" to this process? What problems do they encounter in doing so, and how do they address these problems?

Each of the three cluster teams developed and followed its own individual methodology in pursuing its objectives. The best practices and lessons learned that were discovered by the cluster teams were brought to the core team and discussed. Throughout the study, the key challenge was to define what must happen to enable government leaders to manage their work through the use of a balanced set of measures. The report, which represents the team's synthesis of best practices and lessons learned in the area of balancing performance measurements, can be found at the NPR website (www.npr.gov).

This "cross-pollination" approach strengthened the team community of learning and extended it to the sites interviewed. The community of learning created as a result of the study grows as the collaboration on problems, challenges, and best practices in performance management continues.

The teams' experiences and findings form the basis for this book. The team members were invaluable to the author, freely providing their wisdom, experience, and commentary. See Appendix A for a list of team members.

There are some other individuals to whom I also owe a debt of gratitude: to my editor, Beverly Copland, for her guidance and incredible patience with a first-timer; to the *real* experts, Dr. Robert Kaplan, Dr. Karl Erik Sveiby, the Honorable Maurice McTigue, and Dr. Patricia Ingraham for answering all those questions; to Morley Winograd and the crew at the National Partnership for Reinventing Government for their unfailing good grace; to Adel Shalaby, Chief Information Officer Branch, Treasury Board Secretariat of Canada, and Jay Cavanagh, Department of Energy, for their insightful commentary; to John Keith, Bureau of Land Management, for his writing on the public sector value chain; to Sharon Caudle, General Accounting Office, for her material on public sector governance responsibilities; and to Bill Magrogan, Management Concepts, Inc., for his helpful critiques. Finally, with much love to my husband, John, and daughter, Elizabeth, for putting up with me while I put this together; and most of all for my parents, who always believed in me, even when I didn't.

Kathleen Monahan
Springfield, Virginia
November 2000

CHAPTER 1

Introduction to Using a Balanced Approach in the Public Sector

- History of Strategic Planning in the Public Sector
- History of the Balanced Approach
- Application of a Balanced Approach to the Public Sector
- Why a Balanced Approach Works

When the Government Performance and Results Act was first implemented, many felt that government management was somehow "different"—that the same rules that applied to the private sector could not apply to the public, or at least not in the same way. After all, government agencies don't have a bottom line or profit margin. But recent efforts show that is not true. The bottom line for most government organizations is their mission, that is, what they want to achieve.

Like the private sector, they cannot achieve this mission by managing in a vacuum. The roles of customer, stakeholder, and employee in an organization's day-to-day operations are vital to its success—and must be incorporated into that success.

HISTORY OF STRATEGIC PLANNING IN THE PUBLIC SECTOR

The history of strategic planning in the public sector begins on separate paths that eventually merge. The private sector has been experimenting for several years with different types of performance management and measurement. These include, among others, Management by Objective, Zero Based Budgeting, and Total Quality Management (TQM). As these various practices began to show significant improvement for private sector entities, state and local governments began to experiment with them. Frequently led by

1

elected officials with private sector experience, they soon began to develop better communication and management systems.

Federal sector organizations also began experimenting, especially with Zero Based Budgeting and Total Quality Management. The United States Coast Guard acknowledges that its experience with TQM paved the way for its highly successful, continuous improvement and performance efforts today.

> The standard of quality we seek from these actions and the Executive Order is customer service for the American people that is equal to the best in business.
> —*Presidential Memorandum for Heads of Executive Departments and Agencies: Improving Customer Service,*
> *March 23, 1995*

Legislation in the late 1980s and early 1990s began to move the federal sector toward more responsible performance management and measurement. Among the laws and regulations were:

- *Federal Managers Financial Integrity Act of 1982, Public Law 97-255.* Commonly referred to as "FMFIA," the act encompasses accounting and financial management programs and operational and administrative areas and establishes specific requirements for management controls in federal agencies. Agency heads must establish controls that responsibly ensure that: (1) obligations and costs comply with applicable law; (2) assets are safeguarded against waste, loss, unauthorized use, or misappropriation; and (3) revenues and expenditures are properly recorded and accounted for in accordance with the law. Additionally, agency heads must annually evaluate and report on the control and financial systems that protect the integrity of federal programs.
- *Chief Financial Officers Act of 1990, Public Law 101-576.* The CFO Act of 1990 was enacted to improve the financial management practices of the federal govern-

ment and to ensure the production of reliable and timely financial information for use in managing and evaluating federal programs.

- *Government Management Reform Act of 1994, Public Law 103-356.* GMRA furthered the objectives of the Chief Financial Officers Act by requiring all federal agencies to prepare and publish annual financial reports, beginning with fiscal year 1996 activities. At the same time, GMRA authorized the Office of Management and Budget to implement a pilot program to streamline and consolidate certain statutory financial management and performance reports into a single, annual Accountability Report.
- *Government Performance and Results Act of 1993, Public Law 103-62.* GPRA is the primary legislative framework through which agencies are required to set strategic goals, measure performance, and report on the degree to which goals were met. It requires each federal agency to develop strategic plans and a subsequent annual performance plan to provide the direct link between the strategic goals outlined in the agency's strategic plan and the day-to-day operations of managers and employees. GPRA requires that each agency submit an annual report on program performance for the previous fiscal year, reviewing and discussing its performance compared with the performance goals it established in its annual performance plan. The report also evaluates the agency's performance plan for the fiscal year in which the performance report was submitted to show how an agency's actual performance is influencing its plans.
- *Executive Order 12862: Setting Customer Service Standards, September 11, 1993.* This executive order puts "people first . . . ensuring that the Federal Government provides the highest quality service possible to the American people." It requires continual reform of the executive branch's management practices and operations to provide service to the public that matches or exceeds the best service available in the private sector.

All executive departments and agencies are required to "establish and implement customer service standards to guide the operations" of each agency and to "provide significant services directly to the public . . . in a manner that seeks to meet the customer service standard established herein." They are also required to report on Customer Service Surveys and Customer Service Plans.

- **Presidential Memorandum for Heads of Executive Departments and Agencies: Improving Customer Service, March 23, 1995.** With "Setting Customer Service Standards" as the first phase, this presidential memorandum directs that, in order to continue customer service reform, agencies shall treat the requirements of the earlier executive order as continuing requirements. The purpose of this is to establish and implement customer service standards that will guide the operations of the executive branch. "Services" include those provided directly to the public, delivered in partnership with state and local governments by small agencies, regulatory agencies, and enforcement agencies. Results achieved are measured against the customer service standards and reported annually. Customer views determine whether standards have been met on what matters most to the customer, and replacement standards will be published, if needed, to reflect these views. Development and tracking are to be integrated with other performance initiatives. Customer service standards should relate to legislative activities, including GPRA, the CFO Act, and GMRA. Employees are to be surveyed on ideas to improve customer service and will be recognized for meeting or exceeding customer service standards. An important observation is made within this memorandum: *"Without satisfied employees, we cannot have satisfied customers."* It is also recommended that agencies initiate and support actions that cross agency lines to serve shared customer groups and take steps to develop cross-agency, one-stop service to customer groups.

abolish

- *Information Technology Management Reform Act of 1996 (also known as the Clinger-Cohen Act or the CIO Act), Public Law 104-106.* This act repeals Section 111 of the Federal Property and Administrative Services Act of 1949 (40 U.S.C. 759), often referred to as the Brooks Act, and gives the General Services Administration exclusive authority to acquire computer resources for all of the federal government. It assigns overall responsibility for the acquisition and management of information technology (IT) in the federal government to the Director of the Office of Management and Budget (OMB). It also gives the authority to acquire IT resources to the head of each executive agency and makes them responsible for effectively managing their IT investments. The primary purposes of the bill are to streamline IT acquisitions and emphasize life cycle management of IT as a capital investment. The key IT management actions are to require agency heads to design and implement an IT management process, integrate it with the other organizational processes, establish goals for improving the efficiency and effectiveness of agency operations, deliver services to the public through the effective use of IT, prepare an annual report on the progress in achieving the goals, appoint a Chief Information Officer, and inventory all computer equipment and identify any excess equipment.

New, focused requirements under these various laws and regulations caused managers to rethink how they planned their activities and how they defined success.

to make a bill into a law →

One law that made a more powerful impact on this area than any other was the landmark Government Performance and Results Act, enacted in August 1993. Commonly referred to as the Results Act or GPRA, it sets out a schedule for the development of a strategic planning process for all segments of the federal government. The need for federal agencies to develop systems for performance management and measurement began a chain reaction, particularly for those agencies whose principal customers or stakeholders are state and/or local governments.

Those state and local governments who had already put systems into place were "ahead of the game." Those who had not were (or in some cases are now) put into the position of catching up with the others. In a sense, this sequence has given new life to the concept of "best practices." The International City/County Management Association (www. icma.org) sponsors Best Practices Symposia, the most recent of which, *Best Practices 2000: Management Excellence and Citizen Involvement*, took place in the spring of 2000. This is just one example in recent years of the significant amount of give and take between the various levels of government. A community of practice has evolved that allows leaders at every level of public service to learn from the experience of others.

HISTORY OF THE BALANCED APPROACH

In the early 1990s, Robert S. Kaplan and David P. Norton introduced the concept of the Balanced Scorecard[1] to the private sector. Their groundbreaking *Harvard Business Review* article (January 1992) and subsequent works discuss private sector efforts to align corporate initiatives with the need to meet customer and shareholder expectations.

At about the same time, Karl Sveiby was introducing the concept of the Intangible Assets Monitor™[2] to the private sector in countries outside the United States. Both of these concepts create indicators that measure aspects of business. Although they appear similar, the two concepts were developed independently.

> People tend to be loyal, if they are treated fairly and feel a sense of shared responsibility.
> — Dr. Karl Erik Sveiby, *The Intangible Assets Monitor*™

Both the Balanced Scorecard (BSC) and the Intangible Assets Monitor™ (IAM) assume that the performance of an organization should be measured by more than merely the "bottom line." The theory behind each is different, however. (See Table 1-1.)

The IAM sets forth the idea that human knowledge has very little to do with money, as very few people handle money. If people are revenue creators, a planner must come closer to "the source" of their knowledge to measure it more accurately. By measuring closer to the source, it will then be possible to create an early warning system, which is more

---

Table 1-1
Comparison of Balanced Scorecard and Intangible Assets Monitor™

Balanced Scorecard	Intangible Assets Monitor™
Learning and Growth Perspective—Directs attention to the organization's people and structure. Investment here is vital to long-term success.	**People's Competence Assets**—Individual ability to act in various situations, which includes work skill, education, experience, values, and social skills.
Internal Business Perspective—Focuses on how key internal processes of the organization currently work and how to improve them in the future	**Internal Structure Assets**—Patents, concepts, models, and computer and administrative systems created by employees and generally "owned" by the organization. This is the "culture" or "spirit" of the organization.
Customer Perspective—Focuses on customer needs and satisfaction within the limitations of the organization.	**External Structure**—Relationships with customers and suppliers, brand names, trademarks, and reputation, or "image."
Financial Focus—In the private sector, this is often referred to as the "bottom line."	The IAM focuses primarily on the three intangible assets and accepts existing financial indicators.

Handwritten marginalia: financial focus; other ways to measure the performance of an organization; meant to align corporate initiative w/ customers, shareholders expectations; measures aspects of business; shareholders, ~ customers; introspection of the present w/ futuristic aspirations; outlook on customers based on the orgs. limits; more individualistic

oriented to the future than one that relies on the financial accounting system. For this reason, the IAM argues that non-financial indicators are probably superior to financial ones. It focuses primarily on three intangible assets (external structure, internal structure, and individual competence) and acknowledges that financial indicators already exist within the strategy of the organization.

The BSC, on the other hand, sets forth the idea that to develop a long-term plan, organizational leaders must strive to balance four separate but intertwined aspects of the organization's environment. Doing otherwise could produce success in the short-term but would ultimately result in long-term failure. In contrast to traditional measurement systems, based solely on financial information, the BSC sets objectives and measures performance from four distinct perspectives that are equally important: customer satisfaction, internal business, learning and growth, and financial. Together, these perspectives provide a balanced view of the present and future performance of the business.

In the public sector, the financial focus under Kaplan and Norton has sometimes been interpreted as the organization's fiduciary responsibilities to the taxpayer. However, Dr. Kaplan observes in a 1999 article that "the financial perspective provides a clear long-run objective for profit-seeking corporations; however, it serves as a constraint, not an objective, for public sector organizations."[3] The article goes on to describe how financial factors make an impact on public sector planning (see Figure 1-1).

BSC users are likely to develop non-financial indicators that are different from those used with the Intangible Assets Monitor™ and that will also be interpreted differently. The IAM assumes that some of the organization's assets are intangible, and its purpose is to guide managers in how to utilize those assets while increasing, renewing, and guarding them against the risk of loss. The IAM is thus more similar to traditional accounting theory with its balance sheet and income statement than the BSC. The BSC begins from the base of a traditional management information system and adds

Figure 1-1

The Different Themes in Financial and Customer Perspectives for
Public Sector Organizations

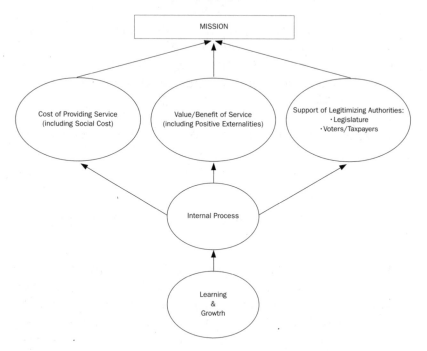

Source: "The Balanced Scorecard for Public-Sector Organizations" by Robert
S. Kaplan

three non-financial perspectives to traditional management
information systems.

While the IAM is based on the "knowledge perspective" of
a firm, the BSC regards the perspective of the firm as a given,
urging managers to take a more "balanced view." In their
1996 book, Kaplan and Norton state: "The Balanced Scorecard complements financial measures of past performance
with measures of the drivers of future performance. The objectives and the measures of the Scorecard are derived from
an organization's vision and strategy." That strategy is then
translated into action through the planning documents.

The BSC takes existing organization theory for granted and then adds non-financial measures to the traditional financial indicators. The BSC can therefore be seen as rooted in industrial-era thinking, arguing that although people in an organization are the first causal step in activities, they are still regarded as costs rather than revenue creators.

The BSC is stricter than the IAM in that it develops very specific links between the measures and the strategy. More important, the two concepts are philosophically different. Unlike the BSC, which is viewed as a tool for management control, the IAM is not about adding another control instrument, nor should the process be used for performance measurement. For such purposes, IAM indicators are too indistinct and easy to manipulate.

APPLICATION OF A BALANCED APPROACH TO THE PUBLIC SECTOR

As a result of these two concepts, a need evolved to study in depth how all these efforts related to the public sector and if they could be replicated there. Could federal, state, and local government entities improve their strategic planning efforts by including customers, stakeholders, and employees in their performance management efforts? What would it take to reach some balance between the needs and opinions of these groups and the achievement of the organization's stated mission?

The IRS learned in 1997 that the measures it was using to encourage performance and to track outcomes were not balanced and could encourage inappropriate responses. Hearings focused on problem cases and testimony from employees who felt pressured to take enforcement actions to meet goals. To correct the weaknesses identified in the existing IRS measurement system, the commissioner established a task force in November 1997 to develop a new system of measures. The new approach to measurement that resulted serves to advance principles outlined by the National Commission on Restructuring the IRS, the National Performance Review's Treasury/IRS Customer Service Task Force, and the Revenue and Restructuring Act of 1998, all of which advocate that the IRS balance its traditional focus on business results with measures of customer and employee satisfaction. Unlike previous measurement efforts, the redesigned measures ensure that customer and employee satisfaction share equal importance with business results in driving the agency's actions and programs.

A balanced approach in the public sector must look at four areas of responsiblity, some of which correspond to the original concepts of the BSC: public governance, operational, supporting, and clientele.

Public Governance Responsibilities[4]

Public governance responsibilities address how we should appear to our customers and stakeholders as policy and resource stewards. The mission of the organization must align itself with its legislative mandates, which will provide the basic information. For the federal sector, congressional consultation is especially vital. Consultation with stakeholders is critical to this process and will identify their key needs and requirements, which can then be integrated into the overall planning process. Duplicate or multiple programs can sometimes be integrated through this process as well. Closely analyzing exactly what the organization must achieve and focusing on the mission can clarify expectations for everyone—stakeholder, customer, employee, and the organization as a whole.

Staff from Fairfax County, Virginia, conducted extensive research prior to embarking on their countywide effort of researching "best practices" from the local, state, and national levels of government. Key to this effort was noting what worked well in other jurisdictions, as well as what could be improved. Based on the study, Fairfax County adopted changes to ensure that goals, objectives, and indicators were linked to convey a comprehensive and consistent strategy for agency performance. The focus of performance management was redirected from evaluating what is done to evaluating performance outcomes.

"law making branch."

As you look for the best policy results and achievement of mission, keep in mind that you are enacting legislative language. Are the mandated policies effectively translated into goals for implementation? Are you also addressing the fiduciary responsibilities of the organization? In a time of budget restraints, it is important to communicate the financial and performance restraints clearly (e.g., an agency is trying to downsize, and there will be fewer individuals to achieve a mission). Figure 1-2 maps out the three phases of strategic planning: (1) defining the mission of the organization; (2)

VISION / visual

Figure 1-2
Balancing the Perspectives

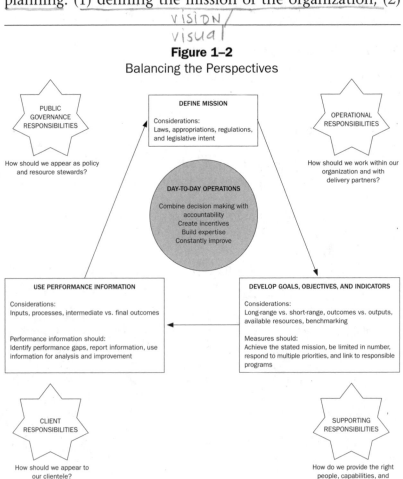

> mission taken shape/
> form/ tangible mission

> (aka)

developing the goals, objectives, and indicators; and (3) using performance information for a continuous improvement process. In your day-to-day operations, continuous
improvement allows you to combine decision-making with
accountability, to create incentives, and to build expertise.
The four areas of responsibility for a public sector organization provide the guidelines for your decisions in this process.

> → performance measures

Operational Responsibilities

Operational responsibilities are how we work within our
organizations as well as with delivery partners, such as state
and local governments, to achieve our stated mission. To be
successful in this area, we must understand and measure
(e.g., for time, cost, quality, and quantity) the core processes
and their value chains. This is an area where "stove-piping"
does the most harm. "Stove-piping" refers to limited or non-
existent communication among individual areas within an
organization. Programs are managed solely in terms of their
impact on the program—that is, within their own cylinder
or stove pipe—rather than in terms of impact on the organization as a whole. In Brazilian culture, management planners refer to a program having "its own church."

As the BSC takes hold, particularly in the federal sector, we
hear about "one" organization, e.g. "One HUD" or "One
VA." This concept of one organization reflects an emphasis
on establishment of cross-program and even cross-bureau
goals and objectives, rather than multiple individual goals.
In some areas where this has been successful, the emphasis is
now shifting to interagency outcomes for future planning
cycles.

The emphasis should be on comprehensive processes and
interrelationships. Process mapping can be a great help here.
Process owners must be identified and held accountable for
the results. Does your organization have delivery partners?
Where do they fit into the achievement of your mission?
Does your service or benefit go directly to the citizen, or does
the funding go through an intermediary source? When you

map the processes, you must include delivery partners and supplier roles.

> Customer consultation played an important role in the development of customer-related indicators for the St. Lawrence Seaway Management Corporation (SLSMC). By agreement with users, certain types of delays (e.g., fog) are not included to calculate transit time achievement. In establishing goals, a "norm" transit time was established, i.e., within normal conditions, as the optimum time to go from Point A to Point B. Transit time targets of 90% transit within norm + 2 hours and 95% transit within norm + 4 hours were then agreed on. SLSMC and its customers review the results and targets yearly and adjust them if necessary. A new customer survey will soon be designed to evaluate better overall customer satisfaction.

Supporting Responsibilities

Supporting responsibilities are those responsibilities we have to our employees. Do we have the right people? How do we, as an organization, provide them with the training, capabilities, and technological support they must have to do the job correctly and deliver high-quality service to the customer?

Client Responsibilities

Client responsibilities address how we want to (or should) appear to those outside the organization. The term as used here encompasses not only customers in the traditional sense but also indirect recipients of services or benefits and the ultimate customer: the taxpayer. In meeting these client responsibilities, balancing can become more like juggling—there may never be a time when everyone affected by a particular program will be in total agreement. A *client* is not always a *customer*, because some organizations regulate as well as provide a benefit or service. The client, too, has some level of responsibility in the achievement of successful results.

Communication among the groups can help define the limitations of the public sector organization, especially for the recipient of the service. The expectations of an individual receiving a benefit or service may be beyond the capabilities of the organization. There must be balance between what the recipient, as a customer, wants and what the organization can provide while maintaining its responsibilities to the taxpayer. Communication can become critical—honesty regarding limitations vs. expectations allows "opposing" sides to understand the strategic planning issues with which the organization is struggling. The client groups, clearly defined, need to be involved in defining goals, targets, and strategies.

> Communications can be conducted more effectively if a strategic approach is adopted. While a communications campaign can be waged on an ad hoc basis, an organization will get a better return on its investment if the activities are undertaken within a strategic framework.

Where does financial measurement fit into this scenario? While public sector organizations do not exist to make a profit, they do have a fiduciary responsibility to achieve their mission in a cost-efficient manner. Measurement of these responsibilities is most clearly defined in such legislation as the Chief Financial Officers Act, the Government Management Reform Act, and the Clinger-Cohen Act. GPRA, too, requires linking budgetary resources with strategic planning efforts. However, financial performance is not the only area that crosses from private sector to public sector.

Customer satisfaction is particularly important to public sector organizations, since one of the customers—the taxpayer—is also the source of funding. While in the private sector, internal efficiency would not generally be of concern to the customer, efficiency and productivity are of great concern to government customers, as they are paying for the service. For this reason, internal efficiency, also referred to as cost-effectiveness, should be a key element in strategic planning in the public sector.

The successful organizations cited in this book believe that, while there is no perfect fit within the public sector for either the Balanced Scorecard as envisioned by Kaplan and Norton or the Intangible Assets Monitor™ of Sveiby, the overall concept can nevertheless be useful in government planning—particularly with some tinkering and tailoring. For example, public sector organizations with the most mature strategic planning processes—notably, city and state governments—feel that the area of employee satisfaction translates better to the public sector when viewed as employee empowerment or involvement.

Some important lessons to remember about balancing performance measurement include:

- *Adapt, don't adopt:* Make a best practice work for you. As you read through the case studies in this book, you will learn what has worked for other public sector organizations. Each organization, whether public or private, has its own unique culture. Take the best practices and adapt them to your specific organizational culture — don't try to force what worked in one place onto your organization without taking that uniqueness into account.
- *We aren't so different after all:* Whether public or private, federal, state, or local, there are common problems and common answers. Defining who the customer is may be less of a challenge for the private sector; otherwise, the issues are markedly similar: opening and maintaining solid lines of communication with your customers, stakeholders, and employees; achieving organizational goals in a cost-effective and efficient manner; and making sure your product, service, or benefit is the best possible.
- *Leadership doesn't stop at the top:* It should cascade through an organization, creating champions and a team approach to achievement of the mission. In a public sector organization, the political leadership will shift with elections. If the head of a department really wants to make a lasting difference, the overall process needs to become an integral part of the organization, not just a product produced by the head office or contractor. If

the process is part of the entire organization, it will attain an enduring sustainability.

The Department of Housing and Urban Development (HUD) established a business and operating plan (BOP) process that allows for a continuous flow of information between headquarters and field offices. BOP development begins with the stated objectives in the departmental strategic plan. The process then incorporates the measures developed as part of the annual performance plan and departmental budget. That document, reflecting all HUD-wide goals and objectives, is sent to the program offices, including those in the field. The field offices then develop their individual business plans based on the BOP.

- *Listen ... to your customers, your stakeholders, your employees and unions:* This doesn't mean send out surveys, collect the paperwork, and put it in some fancy notebook on a shelf in the office. It means communicate with them. Be prepared to listen to what they have to say and to act on it.

In the late 1980s, the Fairfax County Board of Supervisors chartered the Human Services Council, a body of citizen leaders, to establish, review, and coordinate a comprehensive plan for human services. Since its inception, the Human Services Council has championed a more comprehensive approach to analyzing and presenting the county's investment in human services. The council has also championed a focus on performance for individual services and the system as a whole.

- *Partnership* among customers, stakeholders, and employees results in success. Don't tell people what they need, ask them. It works much better.

Performance measures for the State of Iowa encompass a variety of employee, customer, and other perspectives. The State's Council on Human Investment (CHI) is chaired by the director of the Department of Management and includes both legislative representatives and private citizens. Focus groups, citizen commissions, and town hall meetings augment the annual citizen survey sponsored by the CHI. In the annual planning process and the monthly review of performance measures, individual measures are grouped by programmatic perspectives.

WHY A BALANCED APPROACH WORKS

Why should you, a government leader, try to achieve a balanced set of performance measures, or what's often referred to as a family of measures?

Because you need to know what your customer's expectations are and what your employee needs to have to meet those expectations.

Define what service or benefit the customer wants and what the employee needs to deliver that service or benefit. No organization can achieve a mission without the tools to accomplish its daily responsibilities, so human resource systems should use employee surveys. Necessary skills and competencies must be determined through analysis. Once those have been determined, then a curriculum of training can be developed. Management tools, such as appraisals, should align stated goals with actual performance. Workforce size and productivity issues, as well as access to information and technology, are also factors to consider. The resulting organizational culture should support the entire workforce in achievement of its mission.

Tying program results to employee evaluations was already one of the strengths of the Austin performance measurement system. The city then took the idea several steps further.

"Alignment worksheets" were created that will be used for each executive-level employee. These worksheets will link the employee's compensation not only with program results, but also with progress made toward the city's strategic goals and vision. In the next several years, these alignment worksheets will be available to each employee, allowing all employees to see how their jobs contribute to all levels in the organization. The new business planning process also allows employees to help determine new performance measures to use.

Because you cannot achieve your stated objectives without taking those expectations and needs into account.

The success of the organization is determined in large part by the involvement of individual employees in the overall process, their awareness of their roles in the achievement of the mission, and their belief in the vision of the organization. Once you have defined your customer and the expectations of service or benefit, you have a basis for discussion with your employee. Involving employees is critical because they are your front line with the customer. (For a more thorough discussion of involving the employee, see Chapter 4.)

> In Coral Springs, Florida, two elements that have been key to making the city's strategic priorities "real" in the everyday activities of all city employees are : (1) the linkage of each city employee to the strategic priorities through Key Intended Outcomes (KIOs); and (2) the development of departmental initiatives that target resources and focus efforts on the strategic priorities.

Most importantly, because a balanced approach to performance management works.

The BSC helps an organization become aligned on one strategy, eliminating the "strategy disconnect" between leadership and line workers by helping employees understand how they personally can make an impact on the performance of the business. It also allows customers to understand the limitations of an organization and adjust their expectations accordingly. When involved in these discussions, the stakeholder is provided with the full scope of the issues and can work better with the organization toward successful achievement of the mission.

When there is an open line of communication among the organizational leadership, the employee, the customer, and the stakeholder, the entire culture of the organization can change, focusing on achievement of the mission.

> During the implementation phase of planning at the U.S. Postal Service (USPS), strategies are rolled out. Performance is

tracked by performance cluster throughout USPS and publicized, and executive bonuses are based on results.

With the BSC, a public organization has the necessary tools to decide which projects are most important to the achievement of its goals while becoming more efficient and improving the level of service or benefit it is offering to the customer. Most important, the BSC provides a means of communication for successful implementation of strategic plans and a budget that is performance-based.

CHAPTER 2

Determining Public Value: Meeting Public Governance and Client Responsibilities

client?

- The Difference between a Customer and a Stakeholder
- The Value Chain
- The Consultation Process
- Identifying Your Customer and Stakeholder
- Why Regulatory and Enforcement Agencies Are (and Are *Not*) Different

The Bureau of Land Management (BLM) began implementation of GPRA in 1994 by conducting a series of focus groups with stakeholders to determine what measures were important. BLM then established an annual two-year cycle for customer surveys to assess progress on the customer-related performance measures, and an annual employee and customer survey response action plan requirement from all states. Starting in 1997, BLM started using a common set of "mission accomplishment" questions for both employees and customers. Each customer group can be tracked and analyzed by customer satisfaction as related to mission accomplishment. Coupled with the results from the employee survey using the same questions, a direct link can now be made with customer and employee satisfaction with mission accomplishment. For all customer groups, BLM can document that as employee satisfaction increases, customer satisfaction does as well, often point-for-point for all major customer groups. This mirrors the findings of the private sector.

As discussed in Chapter 1, the responsibilities of the public sector organization include public governance and clientele responsibilities. Every organization has a value that reflects its role in society. In the public sector, that value is defined by the organization's mandate and the perceptions of the customer and stakeholder. Public value is created by the satisfaction of stakeholders (such as Congress and the administration) with the outcome achieved as well as the satisfaction of the customer in receiving the desired product, services, and authorization. For those serving in the federal sector, there is added incentive from the Government Performance and Results Act, which requires an assessment of public value. The strategic planning process should be designed to heighten that public value.

To assess the value of your public product or service, you need to create and maintain a dialogue with all those who have an impact on or are involved in any way with the achievement of your mission, including the customer, stakeholder, and employee (see Figure 2-1). This chapter discusses: (1) the definition of public value, (2) the task of identifying your customer and stakeholder, and (3) organization of the process.

On the federal level, the concept of stakeholder consultation for most agencies was previously limited to meetings with congressional staff. Only a limited number of agencies conducted consultation with customers, stakeholders, and employees. Although GPRA was passed in August 1993, the first required document, the strategic plan, was due in September 1997. Most agencies did not focus on their responsibilities under GPRA until fiscal year 1996.

State and local governments, which are not subject to GPRA, have had more time—many of them 10 or more years—to establish, consult, and then redefine their families of measures. For example, the city of Austin, Texas, developed a community scorecard, which includes measures for public safety, crime control, and neighborhood vitality; support of families; and protection of the environment. It also includes shorter term measures drawn from customer surveys that were of immediate concern to citizens. This community scorecard is widely available through the local media and the Internet.

Another successful local government, the city of Coral Springs, Florida, has developed performance measures that

Figure 2-1
Creating Public Value

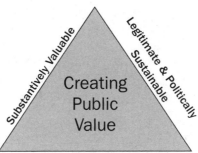

Operationally &
Administratively Feasible

Substantively Valuable—Produce things of value to overseers, clients, and beneficiaries at low cost in terms of money and authority

Legitimate & Politically Sustainable—Ability to attract both authority and money from politically authorizing environment to which it is accountable

Operationally & Administratively Feasible—Authorized and valuable activities can be accomplished by the existing organization or in combination with partners

indicate the city's "stock price." The index includes 10 performance measures most critical to the city's customers (as determined by survey), including residential property values, school overcrowding, and crime rate, and an overall customer satisfaction rating. The city reviews its strategic priorities every two years in formal strategic planning workshops. Management as well as frontline employees and volunteers on advisory boards and commissions have input to the process, which includes financial and demographic data and projections, customer surveys on desires and perceptions, customer input as obtained from neighborhood town meetings, and—of course—performance results. Additionally, each employee of Coral Springs develops personal objectives that tie back to the city's key intended outcomes, thus connecting them to strategic priorities and ensuring that employees actually understand them. All these interconnected processes create a city with a reputation for being an open and caring community in which to live and work.

> In the Fairfax County, Virginia, Department of Systems Management for Human Services, staff solicit feedback on their performance through customer surveys distributed at key project milestones as well as through mid-year evaluation feedback sessions with selected peers and customers.

With the most recent budget and planning cycle, many federal agencies are making a sincere effort to work with their customers, stakeholders, and employees. The consultation phase of performance management and planning is expected to be far more focused in the federal sector as agencies reevaluate their strategic plans and FY2002 annual performance plans, especially in light of progress made with annual performance plans from fiscal years 1999 through 2001.

Legislative support can be a by-product of a successful consultation process — if you make legislatures partners in that process. For example, the states of Texas and Iowa consult extensively with their legislative bodies when developing their priorities.

Natural Resources of Canada credits its success in performance measurement to three factors: top management support, intra-departmental collaboration, and consultation with top stakeholders, including the Canadian Parliament.

Public support, created because the client has input into the process, can be highly beneficial when defending budget requests before a legislative body — yet another good reason to communicate openly with the public.

THE DIFFERENCE BETWEEN A CUSTOMER AND A STAKEHOLDER (client)

In the public sector, how is the difference between a customer and a stakeholder defined? It is not a simple delineation; the boundaries are not clear, bright lines. The dictionary defines a customer as someone who "purchases goods or services from another." A stakeholder is "a person or group that has an investment, share, or interest in something."

The Bureau of Land Management (BLM) conducts continual consultation through the use of focus groups (see Chapter 3). Three groups are identified for external consultation purposes: customers, stakeholders, and partners. By their definition, the customer is the direct recipient of BLM's services.

BLM defines its stakeholders as those people or organizations that have an interest in BLM products or services and supply resources (such as the Office of Management and Budget and Congress). They have an interest in how the products or services are produced or in the unintended results of delivering them. Stakeholders are, according to most definitions, not actual recipients of the product or service of the organization. For BLM, stakeholders include the taxpayer.

Partners are those people or organizations (either internal or external) that help BLM deliver its products or services. These include labor unions, universities, state governments, and private industry.

THE VALUE CHAIN

Figure 2-2 shows the value chain for both a public and private sector organization. Note that the top section of the chain is the same for both organizations, while the variance occurs on the bottom portion of the chain. The private sector focuses on shareholder value, profitability, and customer loyalty, whereas a public sector organization has public trust

Figure 2-2
Value Chain

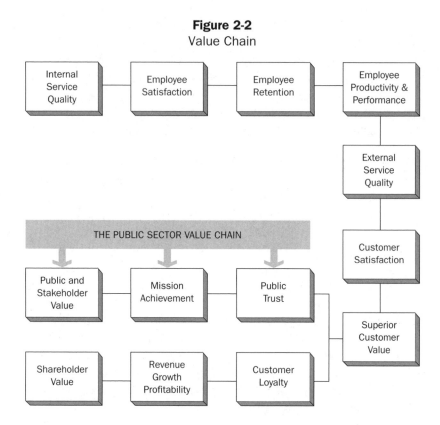

instead of customer loyalty, mission achievement instead of profitability, and public value instead of shareholder value.

Will the successful achievement of your mission create a public value? How do you measure the success of your mission? Do private sector models for customer value translate to the public sector? You need to answer these questions in order to define the *core purpose* of your organization (see Table 2-1). What is the fundamental reason for your existence? The answer lies both in your enacting language and in the minds of those you serve.

In the private sector, major corporations list their core purpose in all their planning documents. Disney will tell you: Our core purpose is to make people happy. For Cargill,

Table 2-1
Core Purpose = Fundamental Reason for Being

Bureau of Land Management	Use and enjoyment of public lands
Forest Service	Care for the land and serve the people
Health and Human Services	To enhance the health and well-being of Americans
Department of Transportation	Ensure a transportation system that enhances the quality of life

it is to improve the standard of living around the world. Hewlett-Packard gives its purpose as "to make technical contributions for the advancement and welfare of humanity." Note the similarities with core purposes in the public sector:

The product or service your organization produces must be:

- *Substantively valuable:* It must produce something of value to the beneficiary at a low cost to the government in terms of money and authority.
- *Legitimate and politically sustainable:* It must attract both authority and money from a politically authorizing environment to which is it accountable.
- *Operationally and administratively feasible:* The authorized and valuable activity can be accomplished by the existing organization or in combination with partners.

In seeking future success for your organization, you should seek out those who have already achieved success and determine what they did right. Success models for BLM and Disney (see Figure 2-3) start with priorities specific to each organization, but neither can achieve success without quality business practices. Those quality business practices reflect your public sector value.

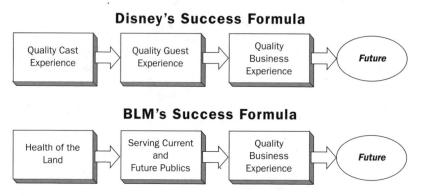

Figure 2-3
Success Models

Disney's Success Formula

BLM's Success Formula

In determining public sector value, there are three traditional options:

- ***Program evaluation***—how well the program achieved its intended purpose
- ***Cost-effectiveness***—how well a particular governmental effort "scored" with respect to a set of purposes and defined effort boundaries
- ***Customer satisfaction***—how well the government effort satisfied the needs of the representative citizens and customers.

A well-structured consultation process will use this third option by establishing and maintaining open lines of communication with representative citizens and customers, including employees and stakeholders.

THE CONSULTATION PROCESS

From mission to measures, a critical part of the development of your plan is to consult with customers to determine what is necessary to satisfy the needs of representative citizens and customers—needs that may be conflicting. These conflicts can be resolved by creating a focus group (see next chapter) with representatives from all points of view, including a stakeholder (who knows the mission of the organization) and a facilitator (to keep things focused), and then listening to the exchange of ideas. Such sharing of ideas and opinions, or consultation, can result in fresh new approaches to old problems.

A distinction between customer and client should be made here. For our purposes, the customer is the recipient of the benefit or service, and the client is any individual citizen who is not a direct recipient. To achieve results, do the customer and client have responsibilities? For example, job training programs are a service provided at many different levels of government. Is it the responsibility of the organization to provide training or to get people jobs? The individual being trained, that is, the customer, has responsibilities as well. A client, the taxpayer, may wish for the responsibilities of the individual being trained to be clarified.

Stakeholders also have expectations, usually based in legislative mandates. They are generally concerned with "the big picture." Expectations resulting from laws, appropriations, and regulations help define the organization's role in society and the impact of the organization's activities.

Employees know what they need to get the job done. Consulting with them helps define those needs, including alignment of goals and human resource systems, access to information, technology, and training. Employee involvement in the planning process creates an organization based on results, which in turn results in higher levels of employee satisfaction and retention.

Consultation has a significant impact on how the organization's overall performance is managed. If your customers, stakeholders, and employees are part of the planning process, they then become part of the achievement as well, building an environment of trust and openness that can make positive changes. The strategic planning process, from establishment to performance reporting, should thus be collaborative and interactive at all levels.

IDENTIFYING YOUR CUSTOMER AND STAKEHOLDER

Defining exactly who the customer is presents a special challenge for government agencies with both an enforcement and service mission, such as the U.S. Coast Guard, because there are essentially two different customer bases. Even regulatory agencies that have a single mission, such as the Environmental Protection Agency, must take into account not only those with whom they deal on a daily basis in their enforcement activities, such as major manufacturers, but also the citizens whom they are protecting with those enforcement activities. And the organization that provides a service or benefit, such as the Social Security Administration, must distinguish between what the customer may want and what U.S. citizens may be willing to spend—that is, to balance their fiscal responsibilities to the taxpayer with their responsibilities to beneficiaries.

The first thing you should do is map out the process completely, from when the dollars are authorized by the legislative body until the product or service is delivered to the customer. If you are providing a financial benefit, such as a voucher, does your organization actually produce the voucher, or does the money go from your organization through intermediary organizations to the beneficiary? Each level of intermediary has an interest in your plans for the future, especially how you prioritize your goals and how you plan to measure your achievements. Process mapping serves a number of purposes: (1) clarifying for everyone involved exactly how your program functions; (2) identifying those affected by or involved in your program at every point; and (3) identifying those areas where efficiencies, when combined with any reengineering or reinvention effort, can most easily be implemented.

Having identified all those involved in the delivery of your service or product, you need to think about how you want to structure your initial consultation sessions. Do you want to have sessions by region, or would you prefer to divide them along issues? Some organizations prefer to organize their larger consultation sessions by an issue, such as welfare-to-work or education. Some federal agencies have held their initial sessions based on a specific strategic goal. Each method has benefits and drawbacks.

If you meet by region, certain areas, such as large cities, may produce such a diverse audience that reaching consensus will be unlikely, if not impossible. In that case, breaking into smaller, more limited groups may be the answer. Avoid holding a session where two large groups with strong opposing views (e.g., a major chemical corporation and an environmental group) are both represented. Putting the two large groups together should be avoided because there is a strong likelihood that the session will be contentious and unproductive. In addition, you want to ensure that the smaller groups and individuals have an opportunity to state their views as well, and not allow the larger group to dominate the session. This is a key role that needs to be clarified with the facilitator.

If you decide in favor of separate sessions with each group, in what order do you want to conduct your meetings? Do you want to talk first with stakeholders, such as OMB, Congress, the state legislature, or local board, and then incorporate their comments and concerns into your proposed plan? Or do you want to meet first with your customers and then take their feedback with you to meet with the stakeholders?

The state of Texas begins the process by meeting with its customers. Once it understands the concerns of the constituency, it then meets with the state legislature. The strategic direction is defined in *Vision Texas*, the governor's statewide strategic plan. The performance measures include both financial and non-financial indicators.

Special interest groups are affected by this decision and may be either stakeholders or customers, depending on how you view their input. Some larger interest groups may be more appropriately considered stakeholders, not only because of the large number of customers they represent, but

dept. that makes or passes a law

also because of their ability to affect legislative decisions. For example, if a plan included a goal to reduce gun violence, the National Rifle Association (NRA) would be a stakeholder, as its ability to lobby could make or break your organization's ability to achieve that goal.

Special interest groups represent a type of customer who should be an integral part of the process throughout. A continuing dialogue with them allows the public sector organization to reach the maximum number of customers in the most efficient manner. They should not, however, become the only contact you have with your customers; rather, you should also allow for individual customer input as well. This is an area where focus groups can come into play.

WHY REGULATORY AND ENFORCEMENT AGENCIES ARE (AND ARE *NOT*) DIFFERENT

prohibited, excluded, restrain from doing or using x w/ authority.

Regulatory agencies face a special challenge in establishing and implementing customer measures. In this area more than any other, the concept of customer vs. client (see Chapter 1) comes into play. An individual who is being investigated, regulated, interdicted, inspected, restricted, or audited will hardly be effusive with customer satisfaction. Some regulatory agencies, therefore, are taking a new look at the definition of "customer," broadening it to include the entire American public. This new focus requires innovative means of assessing satisfaction.

too demostrative expressing excessive emotions

good point

> The U.S. Coast Guard regulates the commercial shipping industry in working toward its strategic goal regarding safety. Shipping companies do not choose to be customers, but because they must comply with Coast Guard regulations and because Coast Guard activities and performance measures are oriented toward safety, they are considered "customers."

In the NPR study, the Regulatory Agencies Team approached the study with the special orientation such agencies have—a recognition of the challenges of achieving com-

to give in / acquiescence

pliance. The team came to realize that regulatory agencies often serve all citizens, thus making all members of the American public potential customers. For example, any citizen who consumes clean air and safe food uses the services of the Environmental Protection Agency or the Food and Drug Administration. The team then searched for different agency approaches to common regulatory problems, looking for such indicators of regulatory culture change as quality of work/life initiatives, analytical tools, and how the agencies identified and met the needs of employees. The team selected a cross-section of safety, commercial, and environmental agencies to represent a broad range of regulatory missions, sizes, and conventions. Following a review of current research in performance, customer service, and management principles, the team identified issues unique to regulatory agencies that are not found in other agencies because regulatory agencies have both "compulsory" as well as "voluntary" customers.

> Its approach allows the IRS to understand both the taxpayer's and the employee's points of view while assessing and improving quality. As a result, the IRS has created an office of "Organizational Performance Management," which helps managers get closer to the work. Among the support activities for this are a "tool kit" for managers and multiple channels for feedback. A tool kit is information provided to an organization that helps the employee/manager do his or her job. In this context, the information would include processes for obtaining customer and employee feedback, as well as the analytical "tools" to analyze that feedback. The integrated operations plan and innovations are being given an opportunity to evolve in a less stressful environment, with temporary suspension of most reviews. The IRS realizes that organizational culture change takes time and that there are constraints on that evolution, including systems and data availability and a need for organizational learning.

Compliance of these compulsory customers *can* be gained voluntarily. Industries can work with regulators, whether formally or informally, to improve compliance. Health professionals, academicians, and other professionals often recognize the benefit in the regulator's products and efforts, whether these benefits are protecting public health, enforcing professional standards, or effecting any other outcomes for the public good that judicious regulation can provide.

However distinct the issues may seem to regulatory and enforcement organizations, the solutions are not always unique. Solutions found by other agencies, such as using the Internet to gather opinions, or using focus groups, can help any organization identify issues important to the customer, client, or stakeholder.

Ultimately, defining your customers and stakeholders begins with where the people are now, not where the organization is going. An organization needs to ask: Who are our customers, and why are they important? What are the needs of each group? What do they look for, and how do we know that? What are our customers' current problems? How will each goal benefit them? One recommendation is to divide both customers and stakeholders by their roles in the process: as doers, supporters, and influencers.

CASE STUDY #1: STATE OF IOWA

The state of Iowa has been designing, installing, using, and refining a statewide performance management system for over four years. It was established through the convergence of a number of forces, including response to public criticism of accounting practices in the early 1990s, broad-based interest in performance-based management, initiatives by state career employees, the leadership of Governor Terry E. Branstad, and the active support of the legislature. These forces, combined with successes reported by some other states, led in 1993 to a legislatively mandated, performance-based management process that is central to the management of state agencies and aggressively involves a wide variety of stakeholders.

Strategic Planning Process

Career employees challenge the process each year, modifying it to meet changing needs and refining it to improve its usefulness. The process has now evolved through four annual cycles, with the final two cycles encompassing virtually every organizational unit of the state government. It reaches from strategic planning activities, through annual planning involving teams of department representatives, to development of the budget.

The mix of performance measures has changed as goals have been achieved or priorities have been adjusted to meet stakeholder expectations. The largest remaining challenge is full integration of the results orientation with the existing line-item budget system, which does not lend itself to measuring results of investments. Until full integration occurs, there will in effect be two budgeting processes running parallel.

Central to the success of the Iowa performance management system is the Council on Human Investment (CHI), which was established by law and initially chaired by the lieutenant governor. It includes four legislative representatives as well as private citizens who have been nominated by the governor and confirmed by the Senate. Senior managers from the executive branch also participate in council meetings. The CHI functions as a focal point for performance management. It receives and analyzes the results of a statistically valid statewide telephone survey of individual citizens on an annual basis. Focus groups, citizen commissions, and town hall meetings augment the design of the survey and the results received from the surveys. The CHI considers these data, performance during the past year, emerging issues, and other relevant factors as it develops and ratifies long-term measurable goals related to overarching issues such as healthy families, economic development, and workforce development. These goals in turn become the umbrella concepts for the state's operating units as they develop their annual plans and address resource needs. The

CHI meets quarterly to review progress made toward the established goals.

Performance Measurement and Management

The CHI as well as the organizational units are using a wide variety of measures and sources. Strategic direction, employee feedback, benchmarks, and goals are typically addressed annually unless circumstances require an intermediate reconsideration. Customer satisfaction is also addressed regularly. Financial, productivity, and performance measures are addressed on a monthly basis. Some indicators, such as internal processes, are addressed on an ad hoc basis. Performance measures, which encompass a variety of employee, customer, and other perspectives, are critical to management of the state's activities. The annual planning process and the monthly performance review, however, tend to group individual measures by programmatic perspectives that include six policy areas: education, accountable government, safe communities, environment, healthy Iowans, and issues related to the workforce and economy. It is important to note that these programmatic perspectives cross organizational boundaries and encourage state agencies to work cooperatively in both the development and achievement of goals. The goals are in turn affected by the development of performance measures in each agency. Each of the 20 state agencies has used from 5 to 10 measures of performance. The state's employees are central to the success of the performance management system. Previous management initiatives (including TQM and reengineering) provided an opportunity for state employees to develop the knowledge, skills, and experience now needed to continue improving performance and accomplishing established goals. The educational and developmental needs of employees and organizations are assessed annually on the basis of the goals and initiatives established during the planning process. The achievement of goals is now widely recognized and applauded, and the state is now considering developing an incentive system for employees.

[handwritten: Possible issue #2— w/ an incentive, employees may falsify results just to get the incentive.]

Leadership

In 1999, Tom Vilsack became Iowa's first Democratic governor since 1968. A former member of the Council on Human Investment, Governor Vilsack has continued to move forward the concepts of reconnecting government with the people through increased public input, accountability for achieving results, and reporting back to Iowans on the impact their government is having.

The Department of Management has initiated a collaborative effort with its legislative counterpart to address the need for a budget redesign. The two key goals are: (1) to meet the needs of customers in both the legislative and executive branches and at the various levels of the decision-making process, and (2) to integrate the results orientation and its measurement component with the line-item budget information needed for cost accounting purposes. *[handwritten: A]*

Lessons Learned

[handwritten: politicians? p.14 client = has some level of responsibility.]

The experience of designing, installing, and subsequently refining the Iowa performance management system has produced a number of insights and learning experiences:

- To be effective, the performance management system must be part of the daily activities of managers throughout the organization and cannot be the property of a particular staff, stratum, or programmatic subset in the organization. *[handwritten: member of a subset of]*
- A performance-based management system consists of a set of activities occurring over time and encompassing a variety of organizations and individuals. All these activities must be aligned so that they support each other.

[handwritten: → necessary to maintain objectivity. → so close to impossible]

[handwritten margin note: always need communi-cation.]

- The quantity, diversity, and consistency of the communication needed to design, install, and operate a successful performance management system is almost impossible to imagine at the beginning of the process. Initial estimates of the effort and energy going into communication will prove to be only a fraction of what is actually required.

[handwritten margin note: Yes- mentioned 2X in the case See A]

- The budgeting process is likely to prove the most difficult process to integrate with a performance management system, (at least in part because of the roles and responsibilities that have been established, practiced, and proven over a long period of time.) ? *expand pls ?*
- For managing for results to be successful, change strategy is critical.

For further information please contact Mary Noss Reavely at the Iowa Department of Management, Council for Human Investment, Mary.Reavely@idom.state.ia.us.

CASE STUDY #2: BUREAU OF LAND MANAGEMENT

The Bureau of Land Management (BLM) manages over 264 million acres of land—about one-eighth of the land in the United States—and more than 560 million acres of subsurface mineral resources. Most of these lands are located in the West, including Alaska, and are dominated by extensive grasslands, forests, high mountains, arctic tundra, and deserts. BLM is responsible for the management and use of a wide variety of resources on these lands, including energy and minerals, timber, forage, wild horse and burro populations, fish and wildlife habitats, recreation sites, wilderness areas, and archaeological and historical sites.

The mission of the Bureau of Land Management is to sustain the health, diversity, and productivity of the public lands for the use and enjoyment of present and future generations.

Strategic Planning Process

BLM began implementing the GPRA requirements in 1994 by conducting a series of focus groups composed of stakeholders to determine what measures were important. From the initial set of meetings, BLM initiated a number of discussions with internal management sponsors (called "strategic basket leads") for each of the major program elements. In concert with the strategic plan development, BLM initiated a customer research program in 1995 to gather internal and external customer requirements.

Based on external and internal customer surveys including stakeholders, and on continued internal discussions and employee feedback, the strategic plan and accompanying performance measures were simplified in 1998 to reduce the number of performance measures from 65 to 45 and the five original goal areas to three: (1) serving current and future publics, (2) maintaining healthy land, and (3) creating an efficient and effective organization.

Of the 45 remaining performance measures, 20% are based on customer survey results. The 2000 Annual Performance Plan proposes a balanced scorecard approach for BLM. Although not included in this plan, more than 25 initiatives are planned to address employee issues surrounding workload management, priority setting, management, communication, employee training, and sagging employee morale and satisfaction.

Introduction of the Balanced Scorecard

Data collection efforts and results indicated that focusing on the customers and employees was a strategic priority in ensuring the successful accomplishment of BLM's mission. This strategic focus precipitated the development of BLM's balanced scorecard as proposed in the FY 2000 budget.

BLM chose to modify the traditional "scorecard" to include a mission element that would provide a link to daily work. The four quadrants of the BLM balanced scorecard are: (1) customer satisfaction, (2) employee learning and growth, (3) financial management, and (4) healthy land.

The strong leadership from the Deputy Director (the highest-ranking career employee) in her current position and formerly in her position as Assistant Director for Business and Fiscal Resources has been the key to BLM successfully developing a balanced set of measures.

The strategic basket leads (program leads) and the field strategic planning and budget leads meet periodically to review the measures and systems. The senior executives have standing working groups to resolve agency-wide strategic issues, to approve and revise existing measures and goals, and to integrate them in the day-to-day processes. They provide employees and stakeholders with opportunities to review the draft plans and measures for GPRA reporting after the work teams have developed them.

They then communicate the results to the stakeholders, customers, suppliers, partners, and others annually based on the required GPRA documents and a combined annual report containing the performance and financial statements. These GPRA documents are made available on the Internet for external review and comment.

The biggest challenge has been in fostering acceptance of the concept and paradigm that employees and customers matter and that being accountable for results matters.

Reinvention at BLM

Based on the 1995 customer and employee survey results, a number of organizational improvements were undertaken, including:

- Six reinvention laboratories (accounting for over $100 million in cost avoidance and savings)
- Reorganization of all offices from three-tier to two-tier

barrier free —
hybridity b/w
agencies

- Establishment of 40 customer service standards
- Establishment of annual customer and employee survey action plans
- Initiation of the Service First partnership with the Forest Service to create a seamless approach to natural resources management (www.fs.fed.us/im/servicefirst)
- One-stop shopping for federal recreation information (www.recreation.gov).

The self-assessment and validation process utilizes a methodology to support and encourage a balanced scorecard approach. Customer service and employee learning and growth are standard elements of interviews and report documentation. Based on the 1995 and 1998 employee survey results, BLM has instituted several organizational improvements: (1) a new employee orientation program, (2) Planned Managers' University, (3) required annual hours of training for managers, and (4) development of a set of core competencies for all advertised managers' positions.

Linkages

The strategic goals are directly linked to the mission statement. The current set of performance measures does not, at this point, direct the allocation of resources. The traditional subactivities from which Congress appropriates still dictate how resources are allocated. However, BLM does associate the strategic goals with subactivities (daily processes that support the overall mission) to ease reporting requirements and show a causal link, collecting more than 300 workload measures for all the subactivities to supplement the performance measures.

Of BLM's three strategic goal areas, two are related to the balanced scorecard: serving the current and future public, and maintaining efficient and effective organization. The customer and the health of the land are explicit in the strategic plan and performance plan, while finances and employees are a subelement of the performance measurement system. Funding for the employees and customers is taken off the top during the budgeting process and is thus linked to the agency's budget and strategic planning process.

BLM has established an annual two-year cycle for customer surveys to assess progress on the customer-related performance measures and a requirement that all states implement an annual action plan to respond to employee and customer surveys. Starting in 1997, BLM started using a common set of "mission accomplishment" questions for both employees and customers. Each customer group can now be tracked and analyzed by customer satisfaction as related to mission accomplishment. Coupled with the results from the employee survey using the same questions, a direct link can now be made between customer and employee satisfaction and mission accomplishment. For all customer groups, BLM can document that customer satisfaction increases as employee satisfaction increases, often point-for-point for all major customer groups. This mirrors findings in the private sector.

BLM has learned through the first years of GPRA that the idea of focusing on customers and employees is not easy to sell to traditional managers and leaders, who do not see collecting data from customers as adding value but as political, and therefore not beneficial to the organization. Leaders need to realize that changes to the organizational culture do not occur overnight but will take time and patience.

Best Practices

Best practices of BLM include:

- Using an integrated, intranet-based, management information system to capture, disseminate, and monitor performance and data
- Establishing employee and external customer research capabilities and having causal baseline and trend information

- Implementing organizational improvements based on employee and customer data
- Tying performance and budget requests and justifications to Congress based on performance information
- Combining reports of performance to the public and Congress
- Integrating the program evaluation system with GPRA and customer research with a balanced measure approach
- Adopting activity-based costing as the method to cost activities, allowing full usage and leveraging of performance data with cost data to make decisions and facilitate the organizational learning of processes
- Linking mission success via customer and employee surveys to establish a connection to the balanced scorecard approach.

For further information, please contact John K. Keith, BLM Management Systems Group at john_k_keith@OR.blm.gov.

CASE STUDY #3: CITY OF CORAL SPRINGS, FLORIDA

The city of Coral Springs launched its quality initiative in 1993, with a mission to be "the premier city in Florida in which to live, work, and raise a family." From the mission, the city commission developed six strategic priorities to focus the daily efforts of all city employees and renewed its efforts to collect data on a variety of performance measures. Three years ago the commission developed its first business plan flowing from these priorities.

Origin and History of Balanced Measures Approach

As Coral Springs applied for the Sterling Award, Florida's equivalent to the Baldrige Award, they realized that their performance measurement was too heavily weighted toward customer "perceptions" and not enough on results. While

Coral Springs continues to track feedback from citizens through a community-wide survey, as well as transactional surveys of service satisfaction, they have worked over the past three years to develop a balanced set of "Key Intended Outcomes" (or KIOs) for each of their strategic priorities.

Strategic Planning Process

The strategic priorities are reviewed by the city commission every two years in formal strategic planning workshops. In the last improvement cycle, staff expanded the input into the strategic planning process to prepare the city commission *before* it is asked to determine its highest priorities. Input from management as well as from line employees and volunteers on advisory boards and commissions, financial and demographic data and projections, customer surveys on desires and perceptions, customer input through neighborhood town meetings, and performance results are collected for the commissioners. The six priorities are: customer-focused government; neighborhood vitality; excellence in education; family, youth, and community values; respect for ethnic and religious diversity; and financial health and economic development.

From these priorities, the city develops a business plan with initiatives that put the priorities into action. The business plan has several key components: an environmental scan, gleaned from the input developed for the strategic planning workshop; a financial plan; and a system of measurement. The measurement section includes all of the KIOs and a "composite index," which was developed to provide a simple "stock price" for the city. Because no other cities have a comparable index, it does not measure Coral Springs' success against others; rather, it measures its success against itself. The index includes 10 performance measurements most critical to the city's customers, including residential property values, school overcrowding, crime rate, and an overall customer satisfaction rating.

The use of performance measures has changed dramatically over the 15 or so years that Coral Springs has employed them. In general, the changes have included employees in their own determination and have simplified the processes. There are now 29 KIOs, as well as 4 to 10 results measures for each department. The KIOs are measures that the city commission has determined are critical to the community's success. The departmental measures ensure a focus on results—and accountability for those results. Department directors meet with the city manager on a quarterly basis to present and discuss these performance measures.

Coral Springs participates in the Performance Measurement Consortium of the International City/County Management Association (IMCA). Collecting and reporting data on ICMA's templates enables Coral Springs to compare its outcomes against a large number of other communities. A quarterly report tracks progress on all departmental objectives. To minimize staff burden for reporting requirements, much of the work has been automated. Each department enters its data into online folders; once all the data have been entered, the report is simply printed and distributed to staff and the city commission. An annual Service Efforts and Accomplishments (SEA) Report is produced at the end of the year to summarize the city's achievements.

Communicating and Using the Data

Coral Springs has invested significantly in sharing its performance results with internal and external stakeholders. The assistant city manager pointed out that Florida has one of the "brightest" of the Sunshine Laws, requiring that all performance data, including employee progress reviews (with employee and public feedback) be included on their individual report cards. Although employees were initially very uncomfortable with this level of visibility, city management decided it was a worthwhile risk because it would build accountability and public confidence in the process. The

State of the City report is released annually at the "State of the City" dinner. City commissioners and all members of city advisory committees, boards, and commissions are invited to the dinner to hear reports on progress in each of the strategic priorities, and future plans for improvement and innovation. In addition to this public celebration, there is an annual Quality Fest for employees, where outstanding individual and team accomplishments are recognized. A bimonthly news magazine goes to every household and often presents progress reports on reaching the city's KIOs, which are posted on the city's website. The site also describes other quality initiatives and awards, including the city's 1997 Sterling Award and most recent first place award in the 1998 Florida Team Showcase.

How the Balanced Measures Are Used and Why They Are Valuable to the Organization

The strategic priorities and KIOs drive the development of the business plan and the departmental budgets. All employees develop personal objectives that relate to the KIOs, thereby connecting themselves to the strategic priorities. Employee reviews include feedback from customers and supervisors, and supervisors' reviews include surveys of their employees.

This linking of each city employee to the strategic priorities through KIOs and the development of departmental initiatives that target resources and focus efforts on the strategic priorities are two elements that have been key to making the city's strategic priorities "real" in the everyday activities of all city employees.

A balanced measures approach has provided accurate trend data and a more well-rounded picture. This allows the city's planning and budgeting to be more proactive, as opposed to the previous approach, which was largely reactive to current customer comments.

Lessons Learned and Next Steps

The city has learned not only from success and state and local recognition and attention, but also from the bumps along the road. The Sterling Award examiners' feedback in their initial application was critical to moving Coral Springs toward a more balanced approach to performance measurement. Making the extra effort to try out new approaches such as the quarterly performance reporting and the ICMA consortium has helped the city develop expertise and fine tune its overall quality initiatives. It has taken time and significant investment in training for them to get where they are now.

One of the most important lessons for Coral Springs has been that, for them, simpler has been better. They have dramatically streamlined the performance measurement process, tracking fewer but higher-quality indicators. The strategic plan and business plan are short, easy-to-read documents. Even the budget has become lighter and more user-friendly.

For further information, please contact Ellen Liston, Assistant City Manager, at egl@ci.coral-springs.fl.us.

The city's website is www.ci.coral-springs.fl.us/CityHall/cm.htm.

CASE STUDY #4: NATURAL RESOURCES OF CANADA

Natural Resources Canada (NRCan) is a federal government department specializing in energy, minerals and metals, forests, and earth sciences. Dealing with natural resource issues that are important to Canadians, NRCan must look at these issues from both a national and international perspective, using expertise in both science and policy.

The agency provides four main services to Canadians:

- Science and technology to provide Canadians with ideas, knowledge, and technologies so that resources are used wisely, costs are reduced, the environment is protected, and new products and services can be created

- Building and maintenance of a national knowledge infrastructure on Canada's land and resources so that all Canadians can easily access the latest economic, environmental, and scientific information
- Ensuring that federal policies and regulations on issues such as the environment, trade, the economy, Canadian land, and science and technology enhance the natural resources sector's contribution to the economy and that these policies and regulations protect the environment and the health and safety of Canadians
- Promoting Canada's international interests, helping meet its commitments related to natural resources, and keeping access open to global markets for Canadian products, services, and technology.

The vision statement for NRCan clearly shows the future direction of the organization:

> As we enter the new millennium, Canada must become and remain the world's "smartest" natural resources steward, developer, user, and exporter—the most high-tech, the most environmentally friendly, the most socially responsible, the most productive and competitive—leading the world as a living model of sustainable development.

In that one statement, NRCan addresses all its public governance and clientele responsibilities.

Strategic Planning Process

NRCan has five major goals:

1. To enable Canadians to make balanced decisions regarding natural resources
2. To sustain the economic and social benefits derived from natural resources for present and future generations

3. To manage the environmental impact of natural resource development and use
4. To contribute to the safety and security of Canadians
5. To manage the department efficiently and effectively.

The last goal includes an employee component and measures. The customer service component is threaded through
all of the goals. These goals were developed based on significant working level discussions, presentations to top management, and stakeholder review. Quantifiable targets are set
for some measures, but several measures are new and need a
baseline established prior to setting targets.

Consultation at Its Best

Canada's Commissioner of the Environment and Sustainable Development, of the Office of the Auditor General, required all federal departments to develop performance measures as part of their sustainable development strategies in
1997. What enabled NRCan to make the process successful
was top management support, intra-departmental collaboration, and consultation with key stakeholders.
All employees were invited to participate in workshops,
with the core group expanded to the intradepartmental
team. All employees had input into the process, which took
approximately six months to develop a first draft of indicators. A departmental performance measurement working
group comprised officials from all sectors of the department.
The performance measures have been continually evolving
since their initial inception and include 39 as of March 1999.
NRCan's effort to integrate employee satisfaction will
be supported through a government-wide employee survey
to be conducted in Canada, the results of which will be directly linked to the set of balanced measures. NRCan is currently aligning its strategic goals with its budget and resource allocations.
NRCan's website is a fine example of government communication. A wide range of information, including perfor-

mance reports, is readily available to any interested party. In addition to reporting performance on goals, objectives, and measures, it also reports management responsibilities and financial information. Of particular interest is Section VI of the performance report, titled "Supplementary Information." Part A, "Honours and Awards: 'People are Our Principal Strength,'" lists every employee who received any form of recognition during the year, whether as an individual or as a member of a team. Part B is the organization chart, and Part C is a complete listing of contact information, including links to other Canadian organizations. Part D is a subject index, and the last page is a reader feedback form with a mailing address, a facsimile number, and an e-mail address.

The department's Performance Measurement Working Group, consisting of sector representatives, ensures employee involvement. These representatives coordinate input to the development of the indicators within their respective sectors and seek direction and approval from their respective assistant deputy ministers.

The performance information is used for focus group discussions, to develop questionnaires at site, and to get a good sense of what the customers want. A review is undertaken during the annual reporting cycle to consider changes in policy and procedures based on the performance of the organization.

The set of measurements significantly influences resource allocations, resource strategies, and operational strategies. NRCan has designed a process to monitor and report on macro outcome measures, which would include observations of their contribution to the outcome in an anecdotal fashion. The department would not attempt to disentangle the attribution of the department to macro indicators, which are influenced by many factors. NRCan's mission is directly linked to the balanced set of measures. Customer and employee measures are integrated into the performance measurement system.

Best Practices

Best practices include:

- Integrated strategic planning with budget
- Created supportive leadership through involvement and sign-off on requirements
- Developed a customer-focused strategic plan and performance measures
- Aligned strategic goals with budgets
- Involved external stakeholders in extensive reviews of goals and measures
- Created a user-friendly reporting format stating the indicator, what it means, the role of NRCan, and what happens next, helping to clarify the societal outcome and the contribution of NRCan
- Established "directional" targets (i.e., maintaining or improving current performance) for indicators where baseline information is being identified.

For further information, please contact Mark Pearson at mpearson@nrcan.gc.ca. The NRCan website is www.NRCan.gc.ca.

CHAPTER 3

Organizing Your Consultation: Assessing Current Reality and Planning for the Future

- The Strategic Planning Process
- Formulating the Mission Statement
- Focus Groups
- Workshops/Retreats
- Brainstorming
- SWOT Assessments

Even strategic planning requires planning! In developing your goals and objectives and in continuing to monitor the degree of success you achieve, you need to determine how you want to gather feedback from all those affected by your organization. A well-developed plan of action is critical to the success of any organization, providing a road map of where your organization wants to go and the route it will take to get there.

> Planning requires imagination, creativity, and fortitude. Things never go smoothly, so be prepared!

THE STRATEGIC PLANNING PROCESS

Although most readers will have some experience with strategic planning, a basic mapping of the process is nevertheless useful. Figure 3-1 reflects the Performance Measurement Process Map created by an earlier NPR benchmarking study. According to this map, there are seven basic phases to strategic planning:

(1) Define the basic functions of the organization.

Figure 3-1
Performance Measurement Process Map

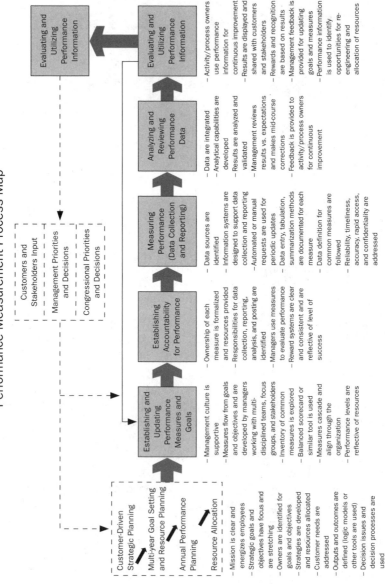

(2) Consult with customers, employees, and stakeholders through focus groups, workshops, retreats, etc.:
- external and internal environmental assessment
- SWOT assessment
- brainstorming

(3) Evaluate the potential impact of ideas generated through consultation on each strength, weakness, opportunity, and threat.
(4) Create a mission, goals, objectives, and strategies.
(5) Analyze the impact of proposed goals, objectives, and strategies on the organization's ability to achieve its basic function (as identified in Step 1).
(6) Finalize and implement strategies, goals, and objectives.
(7) Analyze the impact of the organizational function's actual performance achievement.

By linking decision making with basic organizational functions, an organization creates a framework for making complex, politically sensitive decisions at all levels of the process and at all levels of the organization.

Some basic definitions are necessary.[5]

Strategic planning is a long-term, future-oriented process of assessment, goal setting, and decision making that maps an explicit path between the present and a vision of the future, that relies on careful consideration of an organization's capabilities and environment, and that leads to priority-based resource allocation and other decisions. A well-organized strategic planning system aligns long-range visions, such as mission statements, with the essential levels of short-range functional targets. What results is better teamwork, job efficiency, financial control, and visible performance measures.

Create long-range plans for organizational growth or change. Use an integrated approach that encompasses not only short- and long-range goals but also recognizes the requirements of day-to-day operations. Make the most of limited fiscal resources by not limiting yourself to doing what was done before. Look at alternate methods to implement the planning process. Try to set individual performance targets that align with the strategic direction of the organization. If you do that, individual employees, project leaders, first-line supervisors, and mid-level and senior managers will always know where they fit into the overall plan. As a result of that process, individual and team performance evaluation can become a positive factor, focusing on future activity instead of on a stressful "report card."

Strategies are methods to achieve goals and objectives. They align the organization with the environment in which it must function. Formulated from goals and objectives, a strategy is the means for transforming inputs into outputs, and ultimately outcomes, with the best use of resources. A strategy reflects budgetary and other resources.

Creating an Organizational Vision

It is difficult to determine where you want your organization to be in 10, 20, or 30 years. However, having a vision of the future is what strategic planning is all about. An important element of successful strategizing is understanding the difference between what should never change and what should be open for change.

Vision is a description of a preferred future. Not bound by time, a vision represents global and continuing purposes and serves as a foundation for a system of strategic planning. A vision depicts an ideal future and the contributions that a public sector organization can make to that end.

Formal strategic planning asks and then provides answers to questions of importance in an orderly way, creating a scale of priority and urgency. The process introduces a new set of decision-making forces and tools. It requires management to look at the organization as an integrated whole rather than to plan separately for each component of the business. It forces the setting of objectives for such things as achievement of mission. Future opportunities and threats are clarified.

Through the experience, knowledge, and intuition of managers, combined with the systematic collection and evaluation of data, there is a sharper focus on what lies ahead for the organization.

Mission is the reason for an organization's existence. It succinctly identifies what the organization does, why it does it, and for whom. A mission statement reminds everyone— the public, legislators, courts, and agency personnel—of the unique purposes promoted and served by the organization.

All large private sector organizations perform long-term strategic planning, and an increasing number of smaller businesses are following suit. The same is true of the public sector. GPRA has required federal agencies to follow the path already taken by state, county, and local governments.

Goals are major milestones, usually at the program level. They are the general ends toward which efforts are directed. Goals address issues by stating policy intention. They are both qualitative and quantifiable, but not quantified. In a strategic planning system, they are ranked for priority. Goals stretch and challenge, but they are realistic and achievable.

A goal should need little or no explanation. It should provide inspiration to employees and be tangible, that is, everyone should know when the goal has been achieved. There are some excellent examples to be found in history:
- Put a man on the moon by the end of the decade and return him safely. [Kennedy, 1961]
- Become a $125 billion company by the year 2000. [Wal-Mart, 1990]
- Become the dominant player in commercial aircraft and bring the world into the jet age. [Boeing, 1950]
- Crush Adidas. [Nike, 1960s]
- Destroy Yamaha. [Honda, 1970s]

External/internal assessment is an evaluation of key factors that influence an organization's success in achieving its mission and goals. Detailed evaluation of trends, conditions, opportunities, and obstacles directs the development of each element of the strategic plan. Key external factors may include economic conditions, population shifts, technological advances, geographical changes, and statutory changes. Key internal factors include management policies, resource constraints, organizational structure, automation, personnel, and operational procedures.

Objectives are planned activities that are measurable and time-sensitive (usually one-year or two-year) and that keep the organization moving toward achievement of its mission, as defined through its basic functions. Objectives are clear targets for specific action. They mark interim steps toward achieving a long-range mission and goals. Linked directly to goals, objectives are measurable, time-based statements of intent that emphasize the results of actions at the end of a specific time.

Outcome measures are indicators of the actual impact upon a stated condition or problem. They are tools to assess the effectiveness of organizational performance, public performance, and public benefit derived. An outcome measure is typically expressed as a percentage, rate, or ratio.

Do not discount past planning activities, even if they predate current activities. For example, if a Total Quality Management (TQM) analysis was performed on the annual budget process, there may already be a defined set of key performance indicators. Alternatively, an environmental analysis may have been conducted during a program review or evaluation. All of these can be included in the process without "reinventing the wheel."

The city of Phoenix began developing and implementing performance measures in 1990. The effort is coordinated through the city auditor's office. Phoenix's interest in performance measurement at the time was in part fueled by its interest in total quality management practices and the Government Accounting Standards Board's (GASB) Service Efforts and Accomplishment (SEA) program.

The basic functions of the organization (step 1 above) anchor organizational decisions. The methodology is designed to help decision makers explore and understand the relationships among the organization, the objectives it seeks to achieve, and the environment. Alignment results from analysis of feedback and consultation, including a SWOT assessment (see below). Brainstorming should focus on generating ideas that make strengths stronger and weaknesses weaker, take advantage of opportunities, and neutralize threats.

Ideas generated through consultation should be evaluated in terms of their impact on the organization's ability to achieve its mission. Any form of consultation should be designed to foster communication, analysis, and insight into the organization's daily operations. Those consulted, whether customers, clients, stakeholders, or employees, should understand the plan and their role in its development and implementation.

A manager interested in balancing the strategic process should find a workable, practical way to achieve the desired results while making the most of decreasing resources—both human and monetary.

If management works closely with the employee, they can create a work environment in which all are involved and clearly understand their roles in the achievement of the organization's mission. If individual targets coordinate performance with the mission of the organization, then project leaders, first-line supervisors, mid-managers, and functional executives always know where they fit into the overall plan. As a result, performance evaluation becomes a positive work-focusing activity instead of a stressful "report card."

A balanced approach to strategic planning also improves motivation and morale. If employees have a role in the creation of their own destiny and know what is expected of them, they have a sense of accomplishment when it is achieved.

Increased, open communication with the customer and stakeholder will have a positive effect on their satisfaction with the organization's performance.

FORMULATING THE MISSION STATEMENT

A mission statement captures the essence of why the organization exists and should be a brief statement of organizational purpose. This is an important first step in the strategic planning process.

> Mission statements are created for both internal and external use. Internally, they provide direction and should reflect the organizational vision. Externally, mission statements inform and contribute to an organization's public image.
>
> However, if an organization tries to please everyone, it will please no one. The resultant mission statement ("mom and apple pie") will merely state what the organization has in common with other similar organizations, rather than describing its uniqueness.

To create a mission statement, the participants should consider the question "What is the organization's reason for existence?" The facilitator will probably want to "board" the ideas as they are generated.

Boarding is a method in which each participant is given either a pad of small paper (such as 3 x 3 Post-its) or index cards on which to write down their ideas. A participant records one idea in three to eight words on each card. The facilitator then collects the cards and groups them by common theme, thus finding the vital few most important ideas.

When completed, the facilitator reviews each idea and asks if the concept is actually something for which the organization is responsible or if it is a part of the process toward achievement of the mission. One to five ideas should evolve. They should then be merged into as brief a statement as possible: the mission statement.

Establishing goals, objectives, and strategies forms the basis for your strategic plan. While there is no single strategic planning system that works in all circumstances, the process will include: determining the mission of your organization; developing a profile of your organization that reflects its internal conditions and capabilities; assessing your organization's external environment; analyzing options that match your organization's profile with its external environment while keeping in mind its mission; choosing longer term objectives and the strategies to achieve them; developing annual objectives and shorter-term strategies compatible with the longer term objectives and strategies; implementing strategic choices that match the people, tasks, resources, and reward systems; and periodic review and evaluation.

The size and nature of your organization will dictate the formality of the planning process. A large organization with diversified operations requires a more formal process than a smaller organization whose operations are less complex. Strategic planning is, however, a creative process. If management decides in isolation what the goals and objectives will be and merely asks the next level of management to provide some numbers, the resulting document will be useless and irrelevant. The current reality and organizational culture of each entity is unique, as is its societal role and impact.

Consequently, each strategic plan must be unique and reflect extensive consultation. A balanced approach to consultation and planning is the means to an end. If done correctly, it will result in high performance, good customer service, and trust in the capabilities of the organization, both internally and externally.

One successful method for conducting consultation is to gather a group together for discussion, selecting them according to their interests. After the discussion, be prepared to evaluate and analyze input and report back on the impact of the group's consultation with you. This type of consultation is usually referred to as a focus group.

One successful method for conducting consultation is to gather a selected group together for discussion, selecting them according to their interests. After the discussion, be prepared to evaluate and analyze input and report back on the impact of the group's consultation with you. This type of consultation is usually referred to as a focus group.

FOCUS GROUPS

Focus groups, as defined by the Federal Highway Administration within the Department of Transportation, are a small selected number of individuals who meet to discuss a single topic. Focus groups serve as a tool for gathering opinions and perspectives, and should have the following features: a limited agenda, no more than five or six major questions, not more than 15 people, be organized to gather insights and opinions through conversation and interaction, and involve minimal presentation of material to set context and subject. The Bureau of Land Management also uses focus groups in its strategic planning consultation process.

The informal environment established by a focus group encourages participation. The small size lowers barriers, allowing people to speak out without fear of criticism. Focus groups are not, however, appropriate to all situations. They serve a narrowly defined need for direct and informal opinion on a specific topic. Their special uses include community input from individuals not otherwise represented, gathering expert opinion on a plan, and/or to compare opinions on a concept (e.g., an internal and external focus group). Information from a focus group should supplement other forms of consultation (see Figure 3-2).

Using Focus Groups

Organizing your customers, stakeholders, and employees into focus groups will permit those interested in common issues to provide their feedback at the same time. Focus groups will also help you, as a leader, coordinate responses so that possibly opposing viewpoints may be discussed in the same meeting.

Focus groups should use a facilitator, who is essential to hold the group to the agenda and ensure that each participant has an opportunity to speak. The organization conducting the focus group needs to provide guidance to the facilitator regarding the agenda and purpose of the focus group.

Figure 3-2
Let's Make a Deal

What are we trying to accomplish?
  • A vision of the future
How will we know when we get there?
  • Specific performance measures or conditions that will exist
What is in it for citizens, elected officials and employees? What are the trade-offs?
  • Specific benefits elected officials will derive from the change
  • Specific benefits employees will derive from the change
  • Specific benefits citizens will derive from the change
What is the plan?
  • A 3- to 5-year overview of how the change will unfold
  • Who will lead the change?
  • How will improvements be financed?
  • How will the plan be improved as we learn?

Source: David Osborne. Copyright: The Public Strategies Group, Inc. Reprinted with permission.

A focus group meeting should not exceed two hours and should be scheduled to meet the specific needs of the selected participants. For example, if the organization wants the opinion of working individuals, the meeting should be scheduled for non-work hours, both to encourage participation and to minimize inconvenience to the participants.

On the down side, a focus group only gives you qualitative responses and is not statistically representative of the entire population. It does not meet federal standards for continuing public involvement and cannot replace the more formal process of recording comments and presenting them to appropriate authorities.

A focus group is a discussion carefully planned and used to obtain ideas and opinions on a limited area of interest in a nonthreatening environment. A facilitator is usually used and participation is usually kept to a small number of people. Discussions should be comfortable for participants and encourage them to share their perceptions.

A focus group meeting is a structured process, conducted for the purpose of obtaining detailed information about a particular topic or issue. Focus group discussions are particularly useful in early stages of planning when the precise issues that would permit a more specific research technique (such as a sample survey) may not be known. These types of discussions are also useful both to gather data and to lay the groundwork for more precise evaluation methods.

What a Focus Group Will (and Won't) Accomplish

Focus groups are relatively easy to undertake. They are a good way to "interview" a number of people simultaneously, and results can be obtained in a short time span. The interaction provides freer responses, reflecting the interactive and spontaneous nature of the session. Participants will usually express views that they might not express in other settings, such as when they are interviewed individually.

A facilitator is usually advisable. Guidance should be provided to the facilitator to ensure clarification or greater detail on specific issues of interest to your organization. However, keep in mind that unanticipated lines of discussion may also prove of use to final analysis. Focus groups can work well, not only with a specific population, but also with a diverse one. People who may normally be reticent about expressing personal views often do well in this type of environment.

The capabilities of the facilitator will make a big difference. The facilitator must be able to manage the group discussion while encouraging free expression and a steady flow of ideas. Scheduling can also be an issue. It is sometimes difficult to get all the players in the same location at the same time.

Playing Politics

Another factor that is specific to the public sector can be a very difficult one for management to handle. Sometimes an individual or group of individuals may be reticent to express an opinion in front of representatives of the organization for fear of appearing not to be "team players." They may believe that, if they appear too critical, they will lose their access to the organization's leadership, rendering them ineffectual. Consultation is valuable only as long as the opinions received are honest and open. Reassuring the participants will not address the issue; it is similar to the old adage "we are from the government and we're here to help." (Notice that you still chuckle when you read that, even now.)

There are a number of ways to handle this issue. One way is not to have any organizational representatives at the focus group meeting. If this route is chosen, be sure that the facilitator is completely prepared for the meeting, knows exactly what the priorities are, and yet can be on the lookout for emerging relevant issues.

Another possibility is to provide self-addressed large envelopes with surveys of specific issues of interest to the organization, allowing for anonymous submissions. If this is done, be sure the participants know the time frame in which they must submit their observations.

Analysis and Evaluation

Evaluating the results of the meeting also presents many challenges. It must be remembered that the individual responses were influenced by ongoing discussions and not independently made. Quite a lot of specific information can be generated, making analysis difficult. Also remember that the participants were not randomly chosen, but rather selected based on their interests (and possibly their availability), so do not freely generalize the findings and conclusions.

Defining Participation in a Focus Group

First, ask what the session should produce. Identify the issues for which data should be collected. Once identified, organize the participants, whether employees, customers, stakeholders, or any combination thereof, according to their areas of interest.

Groups should represent specific segments of the population that have an interest in a particular issue. Conditions should promote both comfort and independence of thought, to maximize discussion and self-disclosure. Focus groups should have around 12 members (not counting the facilitator and someone to keep notes). Smaller groups tend to be dominated by one or two people, and larger groups can inhibit participation by all members. A group of around 12 people will usually provide both a variety of ideas and interactive participation.

Conducting the Session

No focus group session should last more than two hours because after that a discussion will begin to lose momentum. The goal is to get as much information on the table as possible. Open discussion should always be encouraged. Group interaction can bring out additional information. The facilitator should stimulate the discussion and keep it on course. Every response and observation should be considered valid. The exercise should be viewed as a gathering of information, with neither support nor criticism of any comment. A session should not try to resolve an issue, address an individual problem or concern, or reach a conclusion.

Summary

Although the presentation of findings will vary somewhat depending on the objectives of the evaluation and the nature of the findings, it is generally useful to present both quantitative and qualitative results. Quantitative results—such as the number of statements that comment on outcomes of asset accumulation or the proportion of comments that are favorable or unfavorable—provide summary information.

Qualitative results can be obtained by using representative comments from focus group participants to create a clearer image of participants' viewpoints. In most cases, the findings will simply report the views of focus group participants as they have expressed them. The strength of a focus group method is that issues can clearly be seen from the participants' perspectives. Comments should meet the following two simple criteria: (1) each is clearly and directly related to the subject discussed; and (2) each makes a consistent point. Comments should be organized to illustrate main themes. Background information and interpretation of findings should be integrated into the report only as appropriate.

WORKSHOPS/RETREATS

Most will agree that strategic planning is vital to a public sector organization's success. A focus group is only one of many techniques that allow a group of people to share opinions and contribute to the development of a strategic plan. A workshop or retreat, usually reserved for internal consultations, is another method of consultation.

As with focus groups, the role of the workshop facilitator is a critical one. There are no right or wrong answers. The most successful workshops allow the participants to explore unlimited options and then select those that best apply to the organization.

The following elements are recommended for a successful workshop:

- There should be a keynote speaker to walk everyone through the overall process and set the tone.
- The workshop should last at least one day, but never more than three.
- Designate a workshop "architect" who will interact with the executive team, helping them to develop and implement a strategic planning framework.
- Designate someone to assess the effectiveness of the current strategic plan, as well as any current processes. (This is usually someone external to the organization who can provide an objective viewpoint.)
- Designate a workshop "coach" who can work with teams to develop and implement strategic planning across all levels of the organization.
- Bring in a professional to design the workshop and serve as facilitator for any planning sessions.

BRAINSTORMING

Brainstorming is a creative facilitation tool that works best with large groups. It is a method that uses combined skills and intelligence. A brainstorming group should concentrate on a specific issue. For the process to work effectively, it is important that the "rules" of brainstorming be followed. It is the facilitator's responsibility to ensure that the process moves smoothly.

The Rules of Brainstorming
There are no "wrong" ideas. Even if an idea seems silly, it may trigger another, more useful, idea in others.
Do not criticize ideas, either verbally or with body language.
Build on each other's ideas. Be creative!
Generate as many ideas as possible within the time provided.
Record all ideas. No one, not even the facilitator, should decide "worthiness."
Periods of silence are okay—let ideas "simmer."

The concept of the "vital few," a product of the quality revolution in the United States, was popularized by Joseph Juran, Ph.D., who drew upon the work of Alfredo Pareto, an Italian economist. The principle of the vital few is that 80 percent of the problems experienced in a process can be accounted for by 20 percent of the core causes. Therefore, if one attacks and resolves or eliminates these "vital few" causes, 80 percent of the problems can be solved.

In strategic planning, there are initially many ideas if a group is determining the strengths of the organization. From that list, 20 percent are selected as the most important. These primary, vital strengths are those that represent 80 percent of the assets of the organization, and thus it is these few strengths that are utilized in the strategic planning process. One way to determine the "vital few" is to ask the group the following question: "If you could count on only X number of strengths to aid the organization in the future, which ones would you choose?"

> As you create an organizational vision, there are some basic questions to be asked:
> 1. What should this organization look like in 10, 20, and 30 years?
> 2. How should our employees and customers feel about us?
> 3. What should the organization achieve?
> 4. If there is a piece in the newspaper or a magazine discussing our organization, what would we want it to say?

The final steps in the above process are integrating the vision statement and the analysis (SWOT assessment, see below), and then identifying the strategic objectives actions that will allow the organization to realize the vision.

SWOT ASSESSMENTS

A SWOT (Strengths, Weaknesses, Opportunities, Threats) assessment views the strengths and weaknesses inherent in an organization and the opportunities and threats that the organization may face. Arising from a variety of trends, strengths and weaknesses are assets and liabilities that are internal to the organization and over which the organization should have control. Opportunities and threats are conditions that tend to be external to the organization and are generally not under the organization's direct control.

Making the SWOT assessment consists of the following steps: defining the business; identifying core competencies, critical success factors, opportunities, threats, strengths, and weaknesses; and assessing current strategies.

The following steps summarize the process:

- Brainstorm all of the issues with which the organization must cope or things it might do in the time frame of the plan. The vision, assumptions, strengths, weaknesses, opportunities, and threats affecting the organization must be clearly defined in order for the brainstorming to have optimal value.
- Discuss and classify each issue as either an end result or as an action to reach an end result.
- Integrate all actions into a coherent and meaningful set of strategies. Many of the items will be subsets or tactics of a larger strategic thrust.
- Integrate the results into meaningful groups. These are the objectives of the organization.
- Prioritize the objectives. Then prioritize the strategies on the basis of the priority of the objectives, and identify what any one strategy will contribute to the accomplishment of any one objective.

At this point, you have the full framework of a strategic plan. The details within strategies are the measures with time frames and identified individual responsibilities for execution.

The SWOT assessment, which can be done by either a focus group or in a workshop, is an effective way to assess the current reality for an organization. The analysis itself, using the SWOT framework, will frequently be sufficient to reveal the type of changes that are necessary to the success of goals and objectives. The following types of questions should be

addressed when conducting a SWOT assessment. Each participant in the discussion should write down individual answers, and then the facilitator can "board" them for discussion. (For an explanation of "boarding," see the section on
brainstorming, above.)

To determine the strengths, decide: (1) What advantages
does the organization have over others that may have similar
societal roles? (2) Which things are done particularly well? In
answering these questions, determine the answers from the
organization's point of view and from the point of view of the
clientele (remember, clientele includes both the customer and
the taxpayer). Don't be modest, but be realistic.

To determine the weaknesses, determine: (1) What things
are not done well by the organization? (2) What improvements could be made? (3) Is there anything that should be
avoided? As with strengths, think about these questions
from both points of view. Sometimes there is a perceived
weakness that will make an impact on the organization,
even if it doesn't really exist. It is especially important to be
realistic about weaknesses and deal with them openly.

Opportunities are determined through the following questions: (1) Where are the organization's best chances for success? (2) Are there new trends or technologies that can help
the organization improve its operations? (3) Is there training
readily available in these technologies for the employee? (4)
Are there recent changes in government (city, county, state,
or federal) policy that have had a positive impact on the
daily operations? Societal attitudes, among other things, can
also provide opportunities for an organization.

Threats are determined by looking at the obstacles to success. For the private sector, the consideration of competition
is vital. In the public sector, this is not the case. Threats to
the public sector include such things as societal attitude and
politics. Is there a member of a city council, county board,
state legislature, or congress who wants to reduce your funding or perhaps eliminate your organization completely? Are
the types of service or benefits the organization provides being redefined or now considered unnecessary by the tax-

payer? Do changes in technology affect how the organization does its job?

Carrying out a SWOT assessment not only serves to reveal
what needs to be done but also serves to put into perspective
the issues and problems facing an organization. For an inter-
esting example of the SWOT assessment, the author—a foot-
ball fan herself—recommends the following website, which
provides a SWOT analysis of the Green Bay Packers: www.
snc.edu/bsad/ba485/spr1998/group4/isw.htm.

A WORD ABOUT PUTTING IT ALL TOGETHER

All the successful organizations cited within this book not
only include the customers, stakeholders, and employees in
their planning activities but also report back to them both
through published reports and the Internet. The importance
of communication is discussed at length in Chapter 5.

General Electric CEO Jack Welch once said, "The winners . . .
will be those who can develop a culture that allows them to
move faster, communicate more clearly, and involve everyone in a focused effort to serve ever more demanding customers." This is as true for the public sector as it is for the
private.

All three elements (customer/stakeholder, employee, and
mission achievement) need to be integrated. This can be
done either incrementally or all at once. For example, an organization may start with the management process, analyzing and improving the internal organization first, then
move to joint accountability and team evaluations. When
that is complete, the organization can move outward, involving customers and stakeholders. Other organizations
find that consulting with the customer and stakeholder first
helps focus the employee discussions.

> The city of Austin uses a family of indicators that measure
> results, outputs, efficiencies, and demands and takes great
> care to ensure that the measurements reflect both the strate-
> gic priorities and the "hot topics" that occupy citizens' inter-

est. The process was initiated about ten years ago to improve government accountability.

Austin's *Community Scorecard* is produced annually and presented to the city council and departmental decision makers. It includes long-range measures, such as improving infant mortality rates, that are linked to each of the four strategic priorities identified in the strategic planning process. In addition to the long-range strategic measures, immediate shorter term measures are included to strengthen the tie to community interests and demands. An example of one such "hot topic" is traffic congestion—an issue very much on the minds of Austin commuters. These short-term measures are determined through comprehensive customer surveys.

However the changes are made and whatever the process is called, to be effective, long-term change and improvement must integrate all of the key areas. Only through a balanced approach to customer service, performance and process management, and employee involvement can organizations become leaders in their fields.

Consultation, whether through focus groups or other methods, should be designed to glean the opinions and expectations of those affected by an organization's activities. Form a partnership with customers, stakeholders, and employees—don't control them. The more an organization forms partnerships with those who have a vested interest in the success of the organization, the more successful that organization is likely to be. Some of the most successful organizations work closely not only with customers and employees, but also with unions and legislators. Better communication results in an increased level of trust.

CASE STUDY #1: U.S. POSTAL SERVICE

The United States Postal Service (USPS) is an agency of 800,000 career and 100,000 temporary employees. Personnel accounts for some 80% of USPS costs, with the remaining 20% divided into approximately 8% for transportation and 12% for rental, services, and others. There are 40,000 post offices, and USPS maintains some 300 plants nationwide.

Historically, USPS measurements were very much internally focused. A tracking system for movement of mail was developed. Under ODIS (Origin-Destination Info System, USPS captured statistics on such outputs as mail movement. In the early 1990s, the dynamics of the market in which USPS served began to change. More competition and the advent of better technology significantly affected their business environment. Under the direction of Marvin Runyon, who became Postmaster General in 1992, USPS began to develop a customer focus. In so doing, they found that many of the measurements they were keeping were not relevant to the customer. For example, they learned that customers placed more value on reliability than on speed.

The new focus caused USPS to re-examine its mission and its relationship with its customers. It began asking questions, such as: What is the nature of our business? What do the customers need and want? How can we get employees committed to the vision? How can we get the organization committed to the employees?

They identified three key "aspirations": business, customer, and employee commitment. From these, the USPS conceived, developed, and implemented a four-stage "Customer Perfect" performance management model founded upon three essential measurement pillars: (1) the voice of the customer, (2) the voice of the employee, and (3) the voice of the business. There should always be alignment among the three, and ideally, the voices of the customer and the employee will dictate the voice of the business.

Accountability

The Customer Perfect management cycle is made up of four phases: (1) establish, (2) deploy, (3) implement, and (4) review.

(1) *Establish:* In this phase, senior management establishes direction, deriving from the various voices the goals, sub-goals, indicators, and targets:

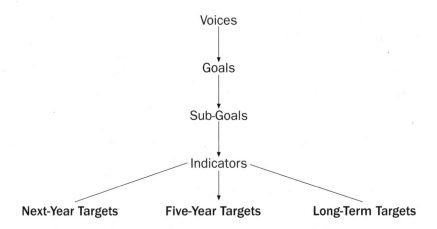

(2) **Deploy:** In this phase, the organization communicates its voice goals, performance goals, and indicators internally. It then aligns programs and activities with the strategic direction and agrees on performance targets, upon which allocation decisions are made.

Budget development is negotiated by means of the "catch-ball" technique, involving the participation of headquarters, the field, and the various performance clusters. Catch-ball is both a top-down and bottom-up exchange.

"Catch-ball" is a child's game where the object of the game is to keep the ball moving, never allowing it to drop out of the player's hands. In this case, it refers to a process whereby an issue (in this case, budget development) is always in someone's hands. Just as in a game of catch-ball, the issue is kept moving and is not allowed to drop.

(3) **Implement:** In this phase, the organization rolls out the strategies it has developed. Performance is tracked by performance cluster throughout USPS and publicized, and executive (SES/GS) bonuses are based on results.

(4) **Review:** There is a continuous, real-time access to and review of performance information. Management reviews performance data and evaluates and validates plans, targets, and programs. Performance clusters (of which there are 85) meeting certain target thresholds are celebrated as "break-

through performers." Employees understand what is important and who is accountable.

Data Collection And Reporting

USPS's experience indicates that a willingness to invest in a performance measurement system is essential. USPS therefore spends $30 million annually on performance measurement systems. Furthermore, because USPS suggests that it is absolutely critical to communicate results and findings to the public, they issue quarterly reports or press releases to the public and quarterly reports to every employee (via the intranet or the union).

An outside consultant does some external measurements, such as audits on the financial indicators. Process indicators are measured daily and weekly within an intranet, organizational database.

In the effort to gauge employee satisfaction, USPS conducts feedback surveys of employees throughout the year, drawing upon random selections of employees. Performance data is available on the USPS intranet.

Analysis and Review

USPS has conducted two Baldrige assessments. The first assessment in 1995 led to the formulation of an improvement plan and the identification of the "voices," which were implemented in 1997. USPS's Quality Department led this effort. CEO/PMG Runyon provided the impetus for the initiative, drawing upon his experience with Ford and Nissan. The challenges, USPS observes, are recording the data, understanding what needs to be done externally, and understanding the nature of the work on a daily and real-time basis. A second Baldrige assessment in 1998 indicated that USPS still needs to make some advances regarding the voice of the employee.

> ### Accomplishments of the United States Postal Service[6]
>
> Achieved fourth consecutive year of positive net income in 1998.
>
> Achieved 15th consecutive quarter of service improvement for local first-class mail, with an overall 1998 score of 93% on-time delivery.
>
> Reduced debt from $9.9 billion in 1992 to $6.5 billion in 1998.
>
> Controlled expense growth to under 5% between 1991 and 1998.
>
> Reduced waiting time in retail units, with 80% of customers served in five minutes or less, and 60% served in three minutes or less.
>
> Consistently improved customer satisfaction measurements.

Evaluating and Utilizing

The chief operating officer is the process owner for implementation of the Customer Perfect. The chief of marketing is responsible for the voice of the customers, and the deputy PMG is responsible for the voice of the employee, as well as Diversity and Human Resources. The Office of the Consumer Advocate works with local and retail customers, and Corporate Relations has responsibility for the general public.

Field offices hold a quarterly celebration for employees when they meet performance targets. The performance clusters are invited to the celebration. A letter is also sent out to all employees announcing who was rewarded and how much they received.

Working and understanding the needs of the customer is the biggest challenge. Account managers have assigned customers and the responsibility for measures for working with them. This is accomplished by establishing partnerships and planning groups to work with participants throughout the value chain (companies, printers, truckers, and sales). These participants look at the surges in business, resources, changes, and impact, always keeping capacity limits in mind.

Strategic Planning

The Vice President for Strategic Planning is the process owner for USPS strategic planning. The USPS strategic plan covers a period of five years and endeavors to understand and position USPS for what the "voices" will be saying in five years' time. The mission is linked to the "voices" as indicated by performance trends. USPS does not issue an annual strategic plan; rather it issues a new strategic plan every few years, depending on the need for course corrections.

Best Practices

(1) *Benchmarking:* benchmarking performance measurement activities with Finland's international postal operations, as well as opportunities within USPS for peer benchmarking and pilot/testing.

(2) *Productivity:* rethinking productivity and determining how best to measure and capture it.

> "The whole mindset at the Postal Service has changed. The battle was how to convince your manager to try something new. Now the battle is to keep up with all the changes your management wants you to implement."
> — Stephen Kearney, Treasurer, USPS

Lessons Learned

Senior management engagement and commitment is essential to successful adoption of robust performance measurement program.

The "catch-ball" technique (top/down and bottom/up internal negotiation) is a valuable tool in the strategic planning process.

Compensation based on performance and measures is very powerful.

It is important to have the organization aligned with the voices and strategic direction.

Communication of performance measurements and results to employees is key.

USPS is beginning to understand internal customer/supplier relationships and is developing agreed-upon internal performance/delivery standards.

USPS created "ramps" for certain bonus thresholds to encourage performing clusters to continue to improve above the threshold.

For further information, please contact Patrick Mendonca at pmendonca@email.usps.gov. The USPS website is www. usps.gov.

CASE STUDY #2: STATE OF TEXAS

A budgetary crisis in the late 1980s, coming on the heels of gubernatorial and legislative reform initiatives, forced Texas to examine ways to allocate resources more effectively and efficiently and prompted the passage of a statute that provided for agency and statewide strategic planning and performance measurement. Further, the state's sustained motivation comes from a desire by policy makers who recognize the need for performance information for decision-making and accountability purposes.

Strategic Planning Process

In Texas, this motivation has been translated into a very mature process that integrates performance measures into the decision-making process. The basic components were developed concurrently in the early 1990s into a comprehensive, interconnected system of strategic planning, performance measurement, performance-based budgeting, and performance reporting, monitoring, assessment, and auditing. Although considered mature, given the extended time in which it has existed as a complete system, it continues to evolve. Interim reviews and evaluations conducted by the governor, legislature, and state auditor, as well as other efforts to build upon and refine the system (e.g., the addition of benchmarking, customer satisfaction assessment, management training, and activity-based costing components), contribute to this evolution.

The state develops these performance measures as part of the biennial strategic planning and budgeting process, and it sets and negotiates them through a formal, though highly participatory, process. Texas is committed to improving the measures over time to ensure that the information needed by decision makers is available.

The performance measures cover the full range of financial and non-financial categories of operational performance, including client outcomes, return on investment, productivity and efficiency, internal processes, customer satisfaction, employee feedback through the *Survey of Organizational Excellence* conducted by the University of Texas, citizen perspectives and feedback, and strategic direction for all functional areas of government through the governor's statewide strategic plan, known as *Vision Texas*.

Performance Information

Texas' use of performance information is the core of a system-wide commitment to innovation and improvement that is highlighted by several Texas-specific efforts, including the governor's Center for Management Development, a state training and education initiative for senior- and middle-level managers; the Council on Competitive Government, which looks at privatization opportunities; and the Incentive and Productivity Commission, which provides cash payments to employees for cost-saving ideas. The State's improvement efforts also include business process reengineering, total quality management, activity-based costing, investment budgeting, benchmarking, and participation in performance measurement consortiums.

This commitment to continuous improvement is also applied to the performance measurement system itself. The process of developing, reviewing, and implementing measures occurs every two years and results in revisions to the state instructions and guides for strategic plans and budget requests as well as the *Guide to Performance Measure Management*. The process is streamlined and updated to ensure that information useful for decision making is included.

Texas believes that the purpose of performance measurement is to provide information for decision making and accountability. Data from the measures is used for strategic planning, annual agency performance plans (operating budgets require performance measures, as do operational plans), resource allocations, and other major policy and operational decisions. Although employee performance plans are made, there is currently no state requirement for them. The legislature is, however, considering a *Texas Performance Review* recommendation to require them.

To ensure that the data are readily available to all decision makers, the budget and performance measurement system is available through an online system. Texas accomplishes this through an automated and integrated accounting, budgeting, and performance measurement system. Agencies enter the information online and report on and update it quarterly.

The Role of Leadership

Key to the success of Texas is the leadership that has been brought to bear on the performance measurement effort by the current and previous governors, top agency managers, and reform-minded legislators, as well as the institutional commitment to training and technical support.

Challenges for the Future

Texas has identified two challenges for its future efforts:

- Ongoing refinement and integration of measures and other data into the legislative and agency decision-making processes
- Improvement in the way state government works with political subdivisions such as counties and cities, the

federal government, subcontractors, and not-for-profits, such as the United Way, as they manage for results in performance partnerships.

Best Practices

Texas brings many best practices to performance measurement, but these two stand out:

- The process is institutionalized, interconnected (i.e., one element or process links to the next), and functional (agencies use data to plan, allocate dollars, and manage). It is part of the accountability and decision-making framework. Planning gives meaning to measures, which also tie to budget. There is a synergistic effect in the linking of efforts.
- There is sustained commitment on the part of elected officials and senior managers.

For further information, please contact Ara Merjanian, Group Director for Planning and Development, Governor's Office of Budget and Planning at amerjanian@governor. state.tx.us. The websites are www.governor.state.tx.us, www.lbb.state.tx.us, and www.sao.state.tx.us.

CASE STUDY #3: CITY OF PHOENIX, ARIZONA

The city of Phoenix began developing and implementing performance measures in 1990. The effort was coordinated through the city auditor's office. Phoenix's interest in performance measurement at its outset was in part fueled by its interest in total quality management practices and the Government Accounting Standards Board's (GASB) Service Efforts and Accomplishment (SEA) program. In 1990, five departments began the process of defining and reporting on a set of performance measures. Each subsequent year, an additional five departments followed suit, until by 1995 all 25 city departments were in some way implementing performance measurements. Despite having been engaged at some level in performance measurement for almost ten years, one official described their efforts as still essentially in the "toddler" phase. Many of the outcome measures are still focused on activities, and there is much to learn and improve upon to make their measurement effort a more systematic, useful component of their decision-making and resource allocations.

The Strategic Planning Process

Phoenix is not formally pursuing a balanced scorecard approach to performance measurement, that is, they do not categorize measures according to the four "perspectives" typically associated with a balanced scorecard: financial, customer, internal business processes, and learning and growth. Instead, they have given their 25 departments considerable flexibility in choosing the performance measures, and how many of them, that are most useful for their particular needs. These measures focus on four performance aspects: (1) customer/citizen satisfaction, (2) unit cost/efficiency, (3) cycle time, and (4) mission accomplishment. The most emphasized of these is customer/citizen satisfaction. Given the leeway granted to departments in defining and using their own measures, not every department decides to use measures focused on each of these four aspects.

Use and Value of the Approach to the City

Phoenix uses performance information essentially for two purposes: (1) to communicate the performance information to elected officials and the public, and (2) as criteria in city managers' personal performance achievement plans. It uses performance data for quality improvement efforts occurs on an *ad hoc* basis at the departmental level, typically after program improvements are identified through other means.

The city of Phoenix's performance measurement effort has provided value to the city in the following ways:

- The city is much more able to respond effectively to information requests from elected officials, citizens, and other stakeholders since they began to track performance data regularly. Prior to implementing the measurement system, performance data was collected on an "ad hoc" basis, making quality responses to information requests more difficult.
- Overall citizen satisfaction and support continues to be high and has improved for the past five years. While it is difficult to attribute this directly to the city's performance measurement efforts, the interviewee believes that it has played some role.
- The regular measuring of performance has created and supported a work environment in which improvement and results matter. While performance data cannot always be tied directly to innovation and improvement efforts, this general environment is consistent with one of Phoenix's core values: a focus on results.

Core values reflect the individuals within the organization, especially the values of the leaders of the organization. To define core values, discuss the following questions, either in a meeting setting or perhaps in a workshop:
  - What core values do you bring to work? These are values that are so basic that they you would practice them whether or not they were rewarded.
  - What core values do you hope your children will hold when they go to work?
  - Do you believe that these values are so basic that they would be valid in any circumstances?
  - What would happen to these values if they interfered with the achievement of the organization's mission?
  - Which values would be basic to every organization, everywhere?

Lessons Learned

Two of the more significant lessons learned concern the decentralization of Phoenix's approach and the frequency with which data can be used. In regard to the former, the city's first foray into performance measurement was characterized by a relatively top-down, centralized approach. This included mandates on how to define measures and in some cases which measures to use. City management quickly encountered stiff resistance to this approach and has since pursued the more flexible, department-driven approach described above. Asking departmental managers to use only those measures they perceive to be functional in their particular context has facilitated both citywide buy-in and the use of more relevant measures. According to the interviewee, had the city not shifted their approach but continued with a top-down strategy, the city would likely have had little success with performance measurement.

Secondly, city staff have recognized that certain data can only be collected on an annual or even longer term basis. In these cases, city staff have been forced to view performance from a longer term perspective and to modify their expectations and planned use of the data accordingly.

For further information, please contact Bob Wingenroth, City Auditor's Office, at bwingenr@ci.phoenix.az.us. The city's website is www.ci.phoenix.az.us/CITYGOV.

CHAPTER 4

Consultation at Its Best: Involving Everyone in the Process

- Listening to Your Customers and Stakeholders
- Consulting with Legislative Bodies
- Listening to Your Employees
- Partnering with Unions

Form partnerships with customers, stakeholders, and employees; don't control. The more you partner with those who have a vested interest in the success of the organization, the more successful that organization is likely to be. Some of the most successful organizations work closely not only with customers and employees but also with unions and legislators. Better communication results in an increased level of trust.

Successful public sector organizations:

- Communicate regularly with employees, customers, and stakeholders
- Use self-assessment tools, such as the Baldrige criteria.
- Involve the legislative branch through consultation or representation on working groups and committees
- Involve the customer, stakeholder, and employee at every phase of the management process
- Involve the unions early and often.

A strategy is a shared understanding about how a goal is to be reached, and a balanced approach allows management to communicate that strategy clearly to customers and employees. Objectives translate into a system of performance measurements that communicates a powerful, forward-looking, strategic focus to everyone. That line of communication begins with well-organized consultation.

LISTENING TO YOUR CUSTOMERS AND STAKEHOLDERS

Once an organization has opened the doors to communication with customers and stakeholders regarding performance management, it is vital that it maintain the flow of information. The customer who has been involved in the planning process will want to know how things are going. The more informed the stakeholders are, the more feedback an organization will receive in the next round of planning—and the better that planning will be as a consequence.

No matter how many focus groups or other types of consultation sessions are held, they will never include the views of everyone. The individual on the street can sometimes provide that one idea that had been missing all along! Don't discount that viewpoint.

> At the U.S. Postal Service, focus on the customer has been the primary driver for its restructuring. Improved performance and internal management emphasize the importance of the customer.

Realize that not everyone is on the Web. This is especially important for headquarters personnel. There is a "within the beltway" mentality, especially in the federal sector, that assumes that everyone is on the web. Those who work in the field offices generally know that if you want to reach the man or woman on the street, you need to use other media as well.

> Coral Springs, Florida, publishes its performance report and makes sure that the local newspapers cover the story. A tireless communicator, the city serves up information and food at an annual dinner, where it unveils its "State of the City" report to its advisory committees, boards, and commissions. Coral Springs also produces an end-of-year Service Efforts and Accomplishments Report; sends bimonthly news magazines to each household; posts key intended outcomes, quality initiatives, and awards on its website; and holds a yearly Quality Fest to honor employee achievement.

//s b/t private & public sectors

Public support will also be created because the customer has been allowed input into what is needed and how best to deliver it. The customer is also the client and a constituent, and the importance of customer support should never be underestimated.

The public sector organization today is as much a customer-driven organization as a private sector corporation is. The federal sector particularly is striving to create a customer-driven government that works better and costs less. Public sector organizations must demonstrate success in meeting program goals and outcomes. This is a major challenge to today's manager: the need to balance the demand for program improvements with decreasing resource availability. The budget process in the public sector especially is driven by performance, and marginal dollars are given to programs that achieve their stated goals.

in terms of quotas, not quality & customer satisfaction
measurables are non-existent in many agencies.

a way
vate
tors too.
ey aim
max,
fits &
ver
sts.

> The Federal Trade Commission's (FTC) Consumer Sentinel database makes consumer fraud data available to U.S. and Canadian federal, state, and local law enforcement agencies. FTC and 47 other agencies jointly maintain this one-stop consumer information website (www.consumer.gov). The agency measures success by the number of hits on the website and the number of calls to its Consumer Response Center phone lines.

How a customer perceives the organization's performance has become a priority for some public sector organizations. Customer service measures should reflect the factors that are of real concern to the customer.

> The city of Phoenix uses its performance measurement system not only to develop criteria for managers' personal performance plans but also relies on the system as a mechanism for communicating effectively with elected officials and the public. Since implementing this data system, Phoenix can respond quickly and completely to information requests from stakeholders. Previously, data were collected and reported only on an *ad hoc* basis.

culmination?
solification

The use of the Internet is transforming the way public sector organizations and customers interact. The catalysts in many cases are independent technology consultants.

The independent technology consultants create the software programs. These programs provide both the public sector and the customer with the ability to communicate. The public sector organization puts its draft documents on the Internet and the customer (and stakeholder and employee) can review the documents and provide feedback. This also allows for open communication throughout the year, not just at the time of a special meeting.

In developing its strategic framework, a public sector organization should make maximum use of all available communication tools. The strategic framework (see Chapter 7) must address customer service, ensuring that the business strategy is cohesive and customer-focused.

The strategy should be developed within the context of the wider strategy of the organization, responsive to the demands of the customer, client, and stakeholder. It should then be implemented as part of the daily operations of the organization and used to monitor its effectiveness and efficiency.

if it reached its goal   *w/i ∠ time ≤*

CONSULTING WITH LEGISLATIVE BODIES

Externally, support may be gleaned from the legislative branch, especially if they are partners in the process.

Consultation with the legislative branch is often overlooked as part of the process. Keep in mind that a well-informed legislator is able to be more supportive of proposed initiatives when he or she can explain the mission, objectives, and goals that relate to that initiative.

The measurement framework for Natural Resources Canada provides the foundation for all departmental planning and reporting documents. It addresses reporting and performance requirements of the department's sustainable development strategy, federal science and technology strategy, and internal management practices. The department has received special authorization from Parliament to align its budget requests to its strategic goal areas. These strategic goals are cascaded to subordinate components to align budget requests and operational plans.

LISTENING TO YOUR EMPLOYEES

Employees have historical knowledge and experience at the daily operations level. Don't underestimate the importance of this information and expertise. Keep in mind that establishing communication is not an overnight process. Simply saying you are going to work with the employee with whatever phrase you choose—consult with, empower, enable, team build with—does not just happen magically. For example, the term "empowerment" has become virtually meaningless in the public sector.

The U.S. Postal Service founded its Customer Perfect performance management model on three essential measurement pillars: (1) the voice of the customer, (2) the voice of the employee, and (3) the voice of the business. There should always be alignment among the three, and—ideally—the voices of the customer and the employee will dictate the voice of the business.

Building employee trust is more easily said than done, as most public sector employees have many years' experience with the management idea *du jour*. Introduce and explain the goals of the consultation, making clear that there is a commitment on the part of organizational leadership to make this succeed. Be willing to discuss the commitment to "make it happen" on the part of management and to integrate it into daily operations. Accountability and responsibility need to cascade clearly throughout the organization. Establish an evaluation process based on the performance of both individuals *and* teams relating to stated goals and objectives. Use the performance information gathered to begin the next phase of strategic planning.

When a manager states a desire to *empower* employees and *reengineer* operations to implement some innovative idea, most public sector employees (especially those who have been in public service for a number of years) will view it as the management theory *du jour* and believe that if they pay lip service to it and keep their heads down, eventually it will go away.

The overuse and misuse of different management tools have rendered them meaningless to the employee. When management talks about building a team, it can mean changing the attitudes of employees or using a team or teams to address some issue or issues. On the other hand, it can also mean filling the organization with employee improvement teams or self-directed work teams with no direct supervision. Reengineering can mean anything from a new management information system to radical changes in the daily processes of the organization, including relationships among employees and customers.

> In the state of Iowa, career employees challenge the process each year, alter it to meet changing needs, and refine it to improve its usefulness. The process has now evolved through four annual cycles, with the final two cycles encompassing virtually every organizational unit of the state government. It reaches from strategic planning activities through annual planning involving teams of department representatives to the development of the budget.

The fact remains that truly involved employees will produce better quality service and higher productivity and will be willing to try new things. Most efforts of this type fail because they do not establish the correct groundwork before heading at warp speed to *empower* their employees.

By no means should you confuse empowerment with programs that are supposed to excite employees through an approach not unlike a pep rally, telling them how to do their jobs by things like "we're a team, let's do it right." This approach only shows the employee how little management knows about the causes of poor performance. Research

Quotable for paper 2

shows that most service, quality, or productivity problems originate in the structure and processes of the overall organization, not in the activities of the individual.

Q1

At the Social Security Administration (SSA), the strategic management focus is on "Programs for Objective Achievement (POAs)." A POA is a written plan identifying a set of strategies and "key initiatives," proposed by an executive sponsor (or team of co-sponsors), that leads to the achievement of a strategic objective. The POA reflects the GPRA focus on results and ensures that SSA's activities are tied directly to its strategic plan and APPs. Budget and IT system resources are allocated to those initiatives that are determined to be "key initiatives." This strategic management framework and process allows SSA to evaluate and act upon the plans, actions, performance measures, and targets on an ongoing basis.

Creating an involved, empowered work force takes a lot of work. You need to develop the leadership skills of all levels of management. Training is the key to developing a culture that encourages and supports employee involvement. If employees hear top management asking for their opinion but find their immediate supervisors still behaving as if they have absolute authority, there is little chance of a change in attitude on the part of the individual employee.

Q2

The Veterans Benefits Administration (VBA) involved numerous parties in the establishment of its balanced set of measures: senior officials, staff managers, line managers, customers, stakeholders, employees, and unions. This broad level of involvement has helped shape VBA's success by making everyone a part of the team.

e.g. vaccining should be done last.

Training the employee is also important because poorly trained work teams will hinder rather than help, and processes will either be significantly delayed or full of mistakes. Management expert Peter Drucker says, "so much of what we call management consists of making it difficult for people to work." Managers can "empower" employees until the cows come home, but if the employees are not able to make a difference, they see empowerment as a way of placing the blame on them for the failure of management.

Employees must have analytical skills to evaluate the processes they use and clarify what is expected of them, both by their managers and by customers. To do this, they need training in how to use problem-solving tools and techniques. In determining their expectations, they should know from senior management what improvements or areas of attention are the most important to the organization.

Senior management needs to support training and sharing of information with the employees and be willing to help eliminate any barriers that may be created by the existing culture of the organization. The need for strong leadership is discussed at length in Chapter 6.

The organization needs to help its employees learn how to communicate with stakeholders and customers, both internal and external. They need to understand how perceptions influence communication and responses. They need the analytical tools to identify ways to create mutually beneficial relationships and build rapport with others. These tools are vital if the employee is to represent the organization well.

Information technology makes it possible to keep all employees, both at headquarters and in the field, equally informed about performance data. Most of our research partners use a combination of the intranet, Internet, and e-mail to keep their employees informed and current on organizational performance. Many also use newsletters and hardcopy postings to communicate this information to employees. Our more successful partners make a concerted effort to ensure constant communication with employees. Best practices include using the intranet and Internet for regular information and using supplementary and complementary dissemination mechanisms to ensure delivery of the message. Not everyone has access to the web, and any communication strategy should keep that in mind.

BLM's management information system (MIS), which integrates its performance, budget, financial, activity-based costing, and customer research data, is available to all employees and managers via the agency's intranet. To provide a clear message to the field regarding the organization's goals and targets and how they are measured, the Veterans Benefits Administration uses the balanced scorecard and posts its results on the VA's intranet. The U.S. Postal Service communicates performance throughout the agency. Every region knows what awards and incentives were given and what performance levels were achieved throughout every region.

The Health Care Financing Administration (HCFA) of the Department of Health and Human Services spreads the word about accountability and results through its quarterly publication, *The Goal Post.* This newsletter highlights key performance measurements and timelines.

Natural Resources Canada inaugurated its website by notifying all 3,700 of its employees of the site's existence and encouraging its use. To reinforce this emphasis on utility, the site features both a user-friendly format and explanations of the data it contains and of the agency's role and future.

PARTNERING WITH UNIONS

To paraphrase an old saying: if the union is part of the solution, it is no longer part of the problem. Partnership with the union is especially critical in achieving culture change within an organization.

At the Internal Revenue Service (IRS), accountability is assigned downward. Specifically, managers are held accountable for their unit's performance, and employees' performance evaluations are linked to organizational performance through critical elements and standards that are aligned with the agency's mission statement and the principles of a balanced measurement system. A steering committee made up of top-level IRS managers and the president of the National

Treasury Employees Union meets regularly to review progress and provide direction in the development of the IRS balanced measures system. By involving the union, the IRS ties in every level of employee in the organization.

CASE STUDY #1: SOCIAL SECURITY ADMINISTRATION

The Social Security Administration (SSA) is an independent agency with approximately 65,000 employees. SSA is committed to both the concepts of GPRA and to improving its ability to manage for results on a day-to-day basis at all levels of the agency.

Strategic Planning Process

SSA has ongoing executive sponsorship for each strategic objective, with an internalized process for sponsorship accountability. Process owners and champions are identified throughout the planning process. The Office of Strategic Management developed a planning guide to help support strategic management within the agency.

The strategic management focus is on "Programs for Objective Achievement (POAs)." A POA is a written plan identifying a set of strategies and "key initiatives" proposed by an executive sponsor (or team of co-sponsors) that lead to the achievement of a strategic objective. The POA reflects the GPRA focus on results and ensures that SSA's activities are tied directly to its agency strategic plan and APPs. Budget and IT system resources are allocated to those initiatives determined to be "key initiatives." This strategic management framework and process allows SSA to evaluate and act upon the plans, actions, and performance measures and targets on an ongoing basis.

Establishing a Balanced Set of Measures

SSA has used a large number of output measures since becoming one of the GPRA performance plan pilot sites in

1994. SSA created a workgroup to develop a performance measurement framework and strategic goals, focusing on what was most important for the public and for customers.

During the pilot phase, SSA developed a performance measurement framework that initially aligned with three strategic goals and ultimately broadened into a balanced set of measures and five strategic goals: responsive programs, world-class service, best-in-business management, valued employees, and public understanding. SSA has used a variation of the balanced scorecard concept since 1994.

In developing its first GPRA agency strategic plan (ASP), SSA's executive staff stated that the agency's mission was "to promote the economic security of the nation's people through compassionate and vigilant leadership in shaping and managing America's social security programs," and then went on to develop the current five strategic goals and objectives.

SSA's five strategic goals and objectives, which cut across all programs and encompass all of the agency's administrative activities, are:

(1) To promote valued, strong, and responsive social security programs and conduct effective policy development, research, and program evaluation
(2) To deliver customer-responsive, world-class service
(3) To make SSA program management the best in the business, with zero tolerance for fraud and abuse
(4) To be an employer that values and invests in each employee
(5) To strengthen public understanding of the social security programs.

SSA's planning process includes the development of POAs, which identify the needed resources and link them with the performance targets.

With the focus of planning on performance, the major criterion for approval or continuation of key initiatives is the extent to which they contribute to the achievement of agency strategic objectives. Accordingly, the executive staff considers proposed initiatives based on whether a compelling business case for a proposed or existing initiative has been presented. The business case answers the key question: "Why should SSA do this initiative, in terms of the cost and the intended benefits?" Benefits are presented in terms of the contribution of the initiative to achievement of one or more strategic objectives.

Accountability

An executive sponsor or a team of co-sponsors manages each strategic objective. Sponsors are accountable for achieving progress against measurable results and ensuring the integration of agency activities necessary to achieve the goal.

They are responsible for developing POAs to include development of objectives, performance indicators, annual and long-range performance targets, identification of the gap between current and target performance, proposal of strategies and initiatives to close the gap, and establishment of a team to manage achievement of the objectives.

SSA's approach to accountability is still evolving, but its purpose is clear: to ensure that progress is being made toward meeting the agency's strategic goals and objectives. At this point, the approach includes several mechanisms that collectively keep the agency on track, including:

- *Quarterly Performance Reviews:* Once a quarter, SSA executives from across the agency meet to assess performance in various agency-wide business processes. In these sessions, particular emphasis is on strategic objectives that affect field operations.
- *Additional Performance Reviews:* Additional reviews may be held as needed to focus on progress in accomplishing agency performance goals. Topics may also include setting or reconsidering short-range performance indicators or targets, issues needing resolution that have been raised by executives about individual objectives they sponsor, and introduction of new KIs.

- *Monthly Tracking of Performance:* SSA has an Executive Management and Information System that provides a library of agency-level performance information used by SSA's executive staff to make decisions.

Many SSA components and individuals are involved in the planning process in support of the executive staff and POA sponsors. These include, among others: component planning representatives, component budget analysts, and key initiative team leaders. A budget analyst is assigned to each objective and each key initiative.

Data Collection and Reporting

The objective sponsor is responsible for assuring that a measurement system is in place to yield valid and reliable measures of performance and to identify a timetable for assessing performance.

Performance data for quantifiable measures are generated by automated management information and workload measurement systems as a byproduct of routine operations.

The performance level for several indicators relating to the accuracy of SSA's processes and public satisfaction comes from surveys and workload samples designed to achieve very high levels (usually 95 percent confidence level) of statistical validity.

Customer input comes from a variety of sources, including market measurement surveys, focus groups, comment cards, and feedback to Websites.

Employee input comes from a variety of sources, including employee satisfaction surveys and focus groups.

Each performance indicator is documented with its strategic goal, strategic objective, objective sponsor, definition, use, data source and contact, frequency of reporting, and validity and reliability.

The monthly status of the performance indicators is available to sponsors and their staff on the Executive and Management Information System Intranet site.

Analysis and Review

An integrated evaluation plan ensures that each strategic goal, objective, and agency business process is appropriately evaluated to assess performance. It also ensures that there is no duplication in the evaluation processes and that the proper evaluations are being conducted.

Collecting, Evaluating, and Reporting to Customers and Stakeholders

Customers receive a pamphlet on achievement of customer service standards, "Reports to Customers." The agency's strategic plan, annual performance plan, and accountability report are available to customers on the SSA's Internet website. Employees have access to these same plans and reports on the intranet site.

The strategic measurement framework ensures links between the body of 64 key initiatives with the goals and objectives in the strategic plan and the annual performance plan.

Key initiatives (KIs) are considered agency priorities and are therefore afforded a high priority in determining the work of the Office of Systems. KIs' designations (as Tier 1, Tier 2, or Tier 3) affect the level and timing of Systems' commitment to support them.

During the development of the agency's annual budget, the executive staff makes investment decisions and tradeoffs focused on how best to support the agency's strategic priorities. Objective sponsors then consider the impact of these budget decisions, especially concerning KIs, on their performance targets.

Best Practices/Enablers

True leadership by the executives. Participation by the executive staff in the development of the performance measures for which they will be accountable helps to create ownership. They must be clear about expectations and true champions of the performance objectives they sponsor. However, this is an iterative process of change.

Quarterly executive management meetings. Quarterly management meetings at which objective sponsors report are an effective mechanism to support accountability for performance.

The planning guidance document. The Office of Strategic Management develops an annual guidebook that describes an overview of the planning framework and guides the development and management of agency plans. It provides a consistent process for staff to follow and reduces the learning curve. The planning guide helps drive strategic management throughout the agency.

Knowledge. It helps to continue to train and orient employees at all levels on the strategic planning process. Training and technical support are continually provided to professional staff involved in performance management. The agency also distributes the annual performance plan (to all who work at the headquarters and to all managers) and the Strategic Plan as a reference tool for day-to-day work.

Customer focus. This is the underpinning of agency planning.

Budget and planning post-mortems. These meetings identify planning and budget process improvements for the next annual cycle.

Lessons Learned

Change is hard, but the more you involve and communicate, the more quickly change occurs.

Executives are busy with near-term management. It is important to make the strategic management process as painless as possible so they can also effectively focus on the long term, for which staff involvement and support are key.

Because the program experts in the area you are measuring will be held accountable, they need to be involved.

Champions and process owners are an integral part of the planning process.

experts?

For performance to be used to manage, there needs to be a tie-in to systems and budgeted resource allocation.

Coordination is needed at the executive and staff levels. You must have executive ownership and involvement. Staffs do what their bosses are interested in and what is measured.

For further information, please contact Judy Cohen at judy.cohen@ssa.gov. SSA's website is www.ssa.gov.

CASE STUDY #2: CITY OF AUSTIN, TEXAS

Austin is a large, modern city that is host to both the state capital and the University of Texas. It is also home to an increasing number of high-tech companies and their employees. Austin city government, serving over 600,000 residents, has a reputation for progressive and customer-focused management.

The Community Scorecard

The city of Austin uses a family of indicators that measure results, outputs, efficiencies, and demands. The city takes great care to ensure that the measurements reflect strategic priorities as well as the "hot topics" that occupy their citizens' interest. Started about ten years ago, the process was initiated to improve government accountability.

The city's annual budget includes over 1,000 measures of results, outputs, efficiency, and demands. Because these 1,000 measures are too cumbersome to create an effective communication tool, the city also produces a "community scorecard" of the several dozen most critical performance measurements.

The performance measures used by the city of Austin are balanced to cover a broad spectrum; indicators of financial health of the organization as well as the efficiency and affordability of the services the city provides are critical components. The city does extensive surveys of its citizens and other customers—and of its own employees—to measure satisfaction and to identify emerging issues. Austin benefits from a large, informed, and very interested citizenry. They participate in city government through boards, commissions, and budget proposals.

Other areas included in the community scorecard include public safety and crime control, vitality of neighborhoods and support of youth and families, and protection of the environment. Finally, indicators are included that measure improvement of internal processes.

The community scorecard is produced annually and presented to the city council and departmental decision makers. It includes long-range measures, such as infant mortality, that are linked to each of their four strategic priorities identified in the strategic planning process. Additionally, shorter-term measures of immediate concern to citizens are included in order to strengthen the tie to community interests and demands. An example of one such "hot topic" is traffic congestion, an issue very much on the minds of Austin commuters. These short-term measures are determined through comprehensive customer surveys.

Austin is in its third improvement cycle for its performance measurement initiative. All of the city's performance measures are tracked by its departments and reported annually in the annual budget. In its most recent improvement cycle, Austin has initiated a "business planning" process intended to provide better alignment with the four strategic priorities, as well as to serve as a method of better aligning employees' work with those four priorities.

Employee Involvement

One of the key drivers of this latest change was a question in the annual employee survey that asked each employee if they used performance measures in making daily operations decisions; only one-fourth of the employees indicated that they did most of the time. Austin's top management decided that they needed a system that would provide more meaningful information to line employees through senior management—information that would be useful in everyday decision making.

Tying program results to employee evaluations had already been one of the strengths of the Austin performance measurement system. They now took the idea several steps further by creating "alignment worksheets" that will be used for each executive-level employee. These worksheets will link the employee's compensation not only with program results but also with progress made toward the city's strategic goals and vision. In the next several years, these alignment worksheets will be available for each employee, allowing all employees to see how their jobs contribute to all levels in the organization. The new business planning process also allows employees to help determine new performance measures to use.

The process enjoys strong top management support. This is a city government with a will to be the best, a city government that spawns many innovations and is open to many more.

For further information, please contact Charles Curry, Budget Office, at charles.curry@ci.austin.tx.us. The city's websites are www.ci.austin.tx.us/budget98/coacomi.htm and www.ci.austin.tx.us/news/voice_survey.htm

CASE STUDY #3: COUNTY OF FAIRFAX, VIRGINIA

Fairfax County, Virginia, had for many years included management indicator-type data in annual budget documents and had been recognized by others, including the Government Finance Officers' Association (GFOA) budget reviewers, as a leader in presenting management indicator data in their fiscal plan. A review of the 1998 Budget Plan and Goals by the Office of Management and Budget (OMB) found that while Fairfax County provided considerable data—approximately 1,700 management indicators—almost 84 percent were related to workload or output. While there were some measures of efficiency and a few outcomes, the predominant focus was on counting what was done. Recognizing that efficiency and effectiveness are more useful for program and budget evaluation, the county initiated steps to educate staff on performance measurement. The county then worked with all agencies to develop a family of performance measures that includes input, output, efficiency, service quality, and outcome.

Staff conducted extensive research prior to embarking on this countywide effort, researching "best practices" from the local, state, and national levels of government. Key to this effort was noting what worked well in other jurisdictions as well as what could be improved. Based on this "best practices" study, Fairfax County adopted changes to ensure that goals, objectives, and indicators were linked to convey a comprehensive and consistent strategy for agency performance. The focus of performance management was redirected from counting what is done to more outcome-oriented performance. This expanded performance information was first included in the FY 1999 proposed budget plan. In releasing the budget plan to the county's board of supervisors, then-County Executive Bob O'Neill noted that "performance measurement is an ongoing process, and this first step marks a starting point for more comprehensive performance management." Fairfax County performance management may be found online at www.co.fairfax.va.us/gov/omb/perf_measure.htm.

Pay for Performance

The next step in this comprehensive change was O'Neill's recommendation to implement "pay for performance" for Fairfax County employees. From the spring of 1998 to the spring of 1999, the Compensation Task Force developed and recommended a model. During the fall of 1999, supervisors and employees worked to develop performance elements for every job classification. Performance elements are required to focus on results, are linked to organizational strategies, and are able to measure quantity, quality, timeliness, and cost efficiency. In addition, employees are expected to develop personal goals that are tailored to their agency's strategic objectives and the organizational strategies. Two county agencies have implemented a multi-rater system to provide feedback not only from the employee's supervisor but from peers and internal and external customers as well. In the Department of Systems Management for Human Services, staff solicit feedback on their performance through customer surveys distributed at key project milestones as well as through mid-year evaluation feedback sessions with selected peers and customers.

Even earlier than the countywide move toward comprehensive performance management, county leadership and the human services agencies began developing strategic goals and objectives for the human services system to better identify and meet the needs of the community. Citizens participate in developing policies, goals, and funding priorities throughout this process.

Performance Budget for Human Services: Citizen-Driven, Cross-Cutting Planning and Budgeting

In the late 1980s, the Fairfax County Board of Supervisors chartered the Human Services Council, a body of citizen leaders, to establish, review, and coordinate a comprehensive plan for human services. Since its inception, the Human Services Council has championed a more comprehensive approach to analyzing and presenting the county's investment in human services. It has also championed a focus on performance for individual services and the system as a whole. In the early 1990s, the council and staff developed a series of human services program budgets as a tool to view the human services budget for each agency along program lines, as opposed to by cost centers and individual funding streams. In 1997, the council sponsored the development of the Human Services Performance Budget, which illustrates how the human services system as a whole responds to challenges in the community and works toward a desired quality of life. The performance budgets for FY1998 and FY1999 look across multiple agencies to identify services that have related objectives and performance targets, regardless of the agency that provides the service.

The performance budgets are organized by seven shared community challenges and contain comprehensive information on performance and funding from state, local, federal, and other sources. The community challenges define seven guiding goals that provide an alternative to the traditional agency-by-agency view of the human services system:

- Providing assistance to promote independence
- Ensuring the availability of safe, affordable housing
- Supporting families and individuals in crisis and preventing abuse and neglect
- Responding to threats to the public health
- Responding to crime in the community
- Addressing alcohol, drug, physical health, and mental health issues
- Providing community-wide and targeted supports to prevent social isolation and neighborhood deterioration.

Community Funding Pool

The community challenges have been used as a tool in evaluating the county executive's budget plans and as a framework for reporting on human services efforts and outcomes. Under the framework of the community challenges, a citizen committee (Consolidated Community Funding Advisory Committee, CCFAC) identified priority outcomes for funding community-based programs and services. Each year since 1997 public forums have been held throughout the county to obtain broad citizen input on the most pressing needs.

In addition to the forums, six focus groups were held to gather the perspectives of low-income residents, including recipients of funded services, to identify their needs. From this public input, the CCFAC determines the annual funding priorities for county general funds for community-based services, as well as for federal funds from the community services block grant. In FY 2000, the funding pool process was integrated with the community development block grant process to further streamline the county's mechanisms for planning and funding community-based human service delivery.

The Community Funding Pool application requires that community-based organizations (CBOs) identify the priority areas that their programs address. They must also identify outcomes and performance measures for their services. In collaboration with the Fairfax/Falls Church United Way, the county offers training and technical assistance to CBOs to develop outcome measures and track achievement of program goals.

Building Community Capacity

Fairfax County is moving toward balanced performance measurement through a multi-faceted approach that identifies countywide, agency, employee, and community goals and progress toward outcomes. In this way, the county is building community capacity for a comprehensive performance management system that is responsive and accountable to community needs and citizen priorities.

Researcher: Patti Stevens, Services Integration Manager (psteve@co.fairfax.va.us). County Contact: Margo Kiely, Director, Department of Systems Management for Human Service (mkiely@co.fairfax.va.us).

CHAPTER 5

The Need to Communicate

- Developing a Communications Strategy
- Changing the Management Style through Communication
- Performance by the Organization, Teams, and the Individual
- Town Halls and Other Meeting Alternatives
- Communicating Internally and Externally, and Where to Differentiate
- The Need for Honesty in Establishing Public Trust

"Moms" Mabley once said: "If you always do what you always did, then you'll always get what you always got." Even assuming that you do a tremendous job of formulating your plans and setting and achieving your stated goals, you still need to communicate that success (and any failures) to your customers, stakeholders, and employees. Otherwise, you will "get what you always got"—a feeling of isolation, secrecy, and mistrust, both from the customer and the employee.

Part of the strategic planning process should be a clearly defined communications strategy that is dynamic, frequent, and reflective of the needs of both management and audience. The communications strategy will be used at all phases of the process, initially for consultation in the development of mission, goals, and objectives. After performance information has been gathered and evaluated, the strategy should work to communicate the successes and failures of the organization. Next is another cycle of consultation to improve the process. Then it begins again! With each performance and planning cycle, the strategy becomes more finely honed to serve each audience well, building an environment of honesty and openness.

DEVELOPING A COMMUNICATIONS STRATEGY

Communication is a driver of organizational excellence, where failure is as easy to discuss as success. The principal function of a communications strategy is to get the right information to the right people at the right time to help them make informed decisions regarding the organization's activities (see Table 5-1).

A communications strategy should begin with no assumptions. Do not let organizational decisions get mired in an attitude of "been there, done that." Be aware of the fact that, as a manager, you may not even know what you need. Technology is changing at a rapid rate, but new, fancy (not to mention expensive) products and services are not always the most useful. The public sector manager must trust the judgment of the workforce and common sense instead of relying exclusively on government specifications.

First, determine the current organizational culture. Remember the SWOT assessment discussed in Chapter 4? What tools are currently available to the organization for communication? Where will the different types of consultation work best (e.g., focus group, surveys)? What will success look like, internally and externally?

The overarching challenge of reinventing government is full-time communication. Because of its size and complexity, communication in the public sector is a full-time job. Working for the public sector is not just filling in forms; it is the collective action of dedicated individuals. Government reinvention, when done correctly, produces results and promotes open communication.

CHANGING THE MANAGEMENT STYLE THROUGH COMMUNICATION

Today, successful organizations are doing what was once considered impossible: increasing customer satisfaction,

Table 5-1
Planning a Communications Strategy

A well-planned communications strategy should take an organization

From a place where	*To a place where*
Management "knows best"	Everyone is aware of changing needs
Performance measures are focused on internal controls	Performance measures are based in perceptions of value—to the customer, stakeholder, and employee
Individual units are "stovepiped," with a narrow view of their individual functions; the mission of the organization is secondary	Managers understand how the activities of their individual units make an impact on the achievement of the organizational mission
The role of employees is to serve the organization	The role of employees is to serve customers, be responsible to stakeholders, and partner with each other to achieve the mission of the organization
Resource allocation and budget decisions are the sole prerogative of management	Resource allocation and budget decisions are made openly, based on performance data collection and analysis
All information is held close by management and not shared among units within an organization nor with the public	Information is shared both internally and externally; limitations are based only on individual privacy or security needs

shortening process cycles and response times, reducing costs, and developing innovative new products and services, all at the same time. Not long ago, organizations could succeed by excelling at one or two of these, but the landscape is now littered with the victims of this obsolete thinking. Today's leaders are capitalizing on the changes and challenges facing all organizations by being better, faster, cheaper, and newer than their less nimble competitors.

Transforming a traditional organization to one that's better, faster, cheaper, and newer is extremely difficult. Organizations in both the public and private sectors have built powerful cultures, systems, and practices that may have been pointed in the wrong direction. This is especially true in the public sector, where organizational cultural change must be an integral part of performance management and measurement.

Historically, three types of management decisions were made: internally focused, functionally managed, and management-centered.

Internally Focused Management Decisions

Most decisions about products, services, and organizational direction are made from the inside out. Specialists, technical experts, managers, planners, and other professionals spend most of their time inside the organization pushing products and services out to the customer.

Here, the needs of the organization are put ahead of those people it is trying to serve. John McDonnell, Chairman and CEO of McDonnell-Douglas, once said of the organization's past practices, "we did not always listen to what the customer had to say before telling him what he wanted." This "we know best" approach found many corporate leaders out of sync with their customers, stakeholders, and employees. Their "bottom line" fell significantly, and their customers, treated as a captive audience, found products and services that better reflected their changing perceptions. Similarly, public sector organizations are now finding that the level of confidence in their product or service has dropped for the same reason: We need to learn to ask the customer what they need, not tell them.

Functionally Managed Decisions

Here, individual departments work to optimize their own internal efficiency. Goals, objectives, measurements, and career paths move up and down within the narrow, functional "stovepipes." Functional managers and their employees focus on doing their own jobs or segments of the production, delivery, or support process.

Functionally managed organizations typically reduce service and quality levels while increasing cycle times and costs. Some results of this type of management include an "us-versus-them" approach to communications, fighting for organizational resources, unmanaged gaps between departments that disrupt cross-functional work processes, improvements or changes in one department that impede the effectiveness of other departments, and losing sight of the "big picture."

Management-Centered Decisions

Management's needs, goals, and perspectives are the starting point for all activities. Managers and their staff professionals are the brains, and employees are the hands. Employees serve their managerial masters and do as they are told. Broad business perspectives and strategies, operational performance data, problem-solving and decision-making authority, and cross-functional skills are kept by management.

But the world is now moving too fast to maintain this type of approach, which puts management at the center of planning and coordination. Managers can no longer know enough, fast enough, enough of the time to anticipate enough of the changes that are needed to make the organization better, faster, and more efficient.

Recognizing that organizations sometimes need to reverse direction quickly, many organizations implemented a variety of improvement programs and process. These include:

Employee Involvement and Empowerment: Many training and motivational programs, as well as structural changes, aim to move daily problem solving, decision making, customer satisfaction, and productivity improvement responsibilities closer to the front lines.

Teams: A rapidly growing employee involvement trend uses departmental, problem solving, cross-functional, project, process improvement, planning and coordinating, and self-directed work teams in many combinations and configurations.

Customer Service: Increasingly, organizations are identifying key customer groups, clarifying and ranking their expectations, working to realign the organization's systems customer around those expectations, and training employees to deal with customers more effectively.

Process Improvement and Reengineering: Data-based tools and techniques, flowcharting, and other "mapping" approaches improve processes at micro or departmental levels. In other cases, processes are radically reengineered across vertical departments at macro or strategic levels.

Training and Development: Many executives recognize the need for massive improvements in skill levels throughout their organizations. This recognition is leading to increased technical communications and effectiveness, data-based tools and techniques, process improvement and management, and coaching of skill development.

Technology: Investments in automation, information systems, voice and data communication systems, inventory control systems, and so on are growing rapidly as companies push for higher productivity, faster response times, and improved service or quality.

The organization must align its systems—for reward and recognition, performance management, planning, and information management—to support employee involvement.

Using Data: Too often, systems serve accountants, technocrats, or management. Get the cart behind the horse. Systems need to serve either customers or those producing, delivering, or supporting the products or services of the organization.

The basic problem is that people are visible, but the systems and organizational culture by which group and individual behavior is shaped are largely invisible. So when something goes wrong, it's easy to trace the problem back to whoever touched it last and lay the blame there.

If you put a good person into a bad system, the system will win. This has been proven so often that it has become a truism in the quality improvement field called the "85/15 Rule." The 85/15 Rule states that if you trace errors or service complaints back to the root cause, about 85% of the time the fault lies in the system, processes, structure, or practices of the organization. Only about 15% of the errors or complaints can be traced back to someone who didn't care or wasn't conscientious enough.

> The Florida Department of Environmental Protection identifies, through root cause analysis, the factors having the largest impact on an identified problem and what can be done to lessen the impact of each factor. The first level of analysis consists of analyzing trends and patterns of data to identify the factors having the largest impact on important problems. Level Two takes the analysis a step further by determining what is causing each identified factor so that the appropriate integrated response can be designed, for example, enforcement, compliance assistance, or collaborative partnerships.

Frontline employees often provide excellent service to the customer in spite of, not because of, their organization's support and systems. Given the obstacles present in many organizations, it's a minor miracle that service is being provided at all! But that service is often being provided by caring employees who believe sincerely in the service they provide to the individual.

The assumption that "the workforce is to blame" is based in a common, but erroneous, inclination to place blame by asking "who" rather than "what" went wrong. The resulting organizational culture—a culture of fear, covering your backside, and finger-pointing—fixes blame rather than fixing the problem. If management really wants to find the source of declining service levels, the best place to start is with an honest look in the mirror and not at the individuals struggling daily to do their jobs.

PERFORMANCE BY THE ORGANIZATION, TEAMS, AND THE INDIVIDUAL

Performance in an organization occurs at three levels: (1) the overall performance of the organization; (2) the performance of groups of individuals, whether as bureaus within an agency or as teams with a single focus per team; and (3) the performance of the individual employee.

The performance of each of these levels needs to be communicated externally to the customer and stakeholder and internally to the employee, but the degree of detail in the reporting varies widely.

The overall performance of the organization should be a matter of public record. Achievement of the mission and strategic objectives generally are in annual performance reports and should also be part of the budget documents to let the taxpayer know what is achieved with the tax dollar.

> The Social Security Administration posts its Accountability Report, which includes its annual performance report as well as its performance on its NPR High Impact Agency goals, on its website, *SSA Online*. The agency also distributes periodic Reports to Customers, covering its customer service standards.

The performance of groups of individuals is generally shared with the public but may or may not include individual names. In the late 1980s, the Fairfax County Board of Supervisors chartered the Human Services Council, a body of citizen leaders, to establish, review, and coordinate a comprehensive plan for human services. Since its inception, the Human Services Council has championed a more comprehensive approach to analyzing and presenting the county's investment in human services. The council has also championed a focus on performance for individual services, and the system as a whole celebrates the achievements of their successful team efforts and provides rewards through that system. Competition among bureaus or teams can be a very healthy way to build team spirit and boost morale. The organization should take care, however, to ensure balance, i.e., to make sure that one group doesn't always get the limelight.

Individual performance is not generally a matter of public record. An exception would be when someone does something truly outstanding and deserves special acknowledgment (for example, someone is instrumental in creating a partnership with an outside organization).

A job well done deserves to be acknowledged, so achievements should be shared. Not only does doing so serve to encourage and inspire other employees, it also shows the customer and stakeholder that the organization cares about its employees. But daily performance and achievement of established goals within the performance management process should remain part of the individual's private record.

The sharing of achievements and failures by the organization as a whole, or by groups of individuals, helps foster a new level of trust and communication. This is particularly important in the public sector. There has been a great deal of rhetoric about building the public trust. Polls showed that confidence in the government and in public sector employees to "do the right thing" had dropped to an all-time low. Over the last ten years, with reengineering, reinvention, and the introduction of performance management, that confidence has begun to improve significantly.

Information technology can revolutionize measurement, and investments in information technology free employees to "work smarter." Federal managers need timely access to accurate information. Public sector employees with historical knowledge do not necessarily share that information with managers. Internal communication allows employees to become better professionals, make better decisions, deliver better customer service, meet performance goals, and contribute to an organization's success.

Keep in mind that what you measure is what you get. An organization's performance measurement system strongly

affects the behavior of its managers and employees. Traditional financial accounting measures, if not considered as part of a larger picture of organizational achievement, can give misleading signals for continuous improvement and innovation—activities that today's competitive environment demands.

Since the passage of GPRA, many public sector organizations have tested new kinds of measurement systems that are more appropriate to world-class performance. Most of these performance measures are not new but have been in use in the private sector for many years. What is new is that they can now drive daily operations and decision making.

Here, too, balance is important. Financial measures provide the results of actions already taken. Operational measures complement the financial measures and drive future financial performance. Measures of customer satisfaction are important, but they should measure what an organization must do internally to meet customer expectations. In combination, these measures provide a balanced view of overall performance and bring together in a single report all the functions of a public sector organization. A balanced approach to performance measurement forces management to consider whether improvement in one area may have been achieved at the expense of another.

In developing a performance measurement system, try not to choose between financial and operational measures. No single measure can provide a clear performance target or focus attention on the critical areas of the business. A balanced presentation of both financial and operational measures will provide a more complete picture of achievement.

TOWN HALLS AND OTHER MEETING ALTERNATIVES

With the evolution of the Internet, it has become easy to discount the value of face-to-face encounters. Remember that not everyone has a computer nor access to the web (without going to a local library). The National Partnership for Reinventing Government began a program entitled

"Conversations with America" to engage federal workers in two-way conversations with their customers, the American public, on how to improve customer service. A conversation can take place in many settings: town hall meetings, focus groups, electronic chat rooms, e-mail, customer surveys and comment cards, call-in radio and television shows, and toll-free call centers. For more information on this program, please refer to the NPR website (www.npr.gov).

In Chapter 3, the concepts of focus groups (a small number of individuals focused on a specific issue) and workshops (a large group of individuals, usually concerned with an issue internal to an organization) were discussed at length. Town hall meetings are not a new concept. These types of meetings, based in part on the Quaker culture, have been held for centuries. The term now not only encompasses a group of individuals meeting in a specific location to discuss issues but also refers to linking other interested parties using innovative technology. The basic idea remains the same, however—to reach out to the public and actively seek their input into organizational decisions.

In 1999, the Department of Energy's Yucca Mountain Project (YMP) in Nevada hosted informational meetings in three counties to discuss the Viability Assessment for the Characterization Project and its Environmental Impact Statement. These meetings, announced via local newspapers, mailings, and public service announcements, were held to ensure that project information is shared with the public and that attendees have a voice in the project's process. To ensure an ongoing two-way dialogue on the Yucca Mountain Project, YMP maintains a user-friendly website to collect feedback and offers over 400 interactive tours of its facility each year. By encouraging public interaction and public opinion on projects such as YMP, DOE is working to ensure that its projects receive the public support necessary for efficient and safe operation.

Technology can be useful for purposes of gathering information. Websites and chat rooms can provide meaningful dialogue but should not be the only communication methods used. The National Partnership for Reinventing Government categorized Conversations with America into four areas:

- Face-to-face conversations
- Electronic conversations
- Written conversations
- Telephone conversations.

Chapter 3 included an extensive discussion of the first category. Electronic conversations were discussed above. Written conversations, including customer surveys and comment cards, is an area where the media, especially the print media, can be very helpful. Individuals who may not have a computer will read the paper. Remember that seeking customer opinion marks a significant change in government culture and, although significant strides have been made in recent years, particularly through the efforts of organizations such as the NPR, there is still room for improvement.

Telephone conversations include not only toll-free numbers but also call-in radio and television shows. Toll-free call centers need to be designed and monitored carefully, as few things are as frustrating as being bounced around by recorded voices, asking you to "push 1 now," then "push 7," then "push 2." A personal favorite of mine was the recorded message that ran through all the buttons to be pushed, then added "if you do not have a push button phone, please hold for an operator." Out of curiosity, I held on for ten minutes until another recording told me "this call could not be completed," and the call disconnected! In designing a system, keep in mind that this should be a service—not a contest.

COMMUNICATING INTERNALLY AND EXTERNALLY, AND WHERE TO DIFFERENTIATE

Communication is critical, but is it possible to be too open? Although the public sector may not be prone to "industrial espionage" in the strict interpretation of the term, there are sometimes issues that are inappropriate for a public discussion, perhaps because they contain classified information or will invade an individual's right to privacy. Each organization must evaluate honestly what can be shared with the public and which needs should be kept internal to the management of the organization.

In making this decision, however, management also needs to keep in mind that the more open the organization can be with the public, the better the relationship will tend to be. Overall organizational achievements or failures, as well as team achievements, generally should be available for public review. Sometimes a team may fail to achieve a specific goal, but the learning experience leads to the development of a better process. Learning from one's mistakes shows the customer that the organization is trying.

THE NEED FOR HONESTY IN ESTABLISHING PUBLIC TRUST

A recent presentation by Sharon Caudle, Ph.D., of the General Accounting Office, discussed *public governance responsibilities*. If we, as public sector organizations, are to meet these responsibilities successfully, we must appear as policy and resource stewards to our stakeholders.

In evaluating performance plans and actual performance, the following questions must be answered:

- Is the mission in line with mandates?
- Are key stakeholder needs and requirements understood and integrated?
- Are multiple or duplicate programs integrated for best policy results?
- Are mandated policies effectively translated to implementation goals?
- Are financial and investment performance restraints and expectations made clear?

In an article in the *Harvard Business Review* (March-April 1996, Harvard Reprint 96207), Regina E. Herzlinger observes that trust in major public institutions has been damaged significantly by scandal and general carelessness. Accountability through disclosure, analysis, and dissemination can restore the public trust. Through open communication, the public can see what it is paying for and understand the results of management actions.

> The Commonwealth of Virginia issues a progress report on its performance measures every December. This report, along with planning and budget information, is available both in hard copy and on the Internet.

> The U.S. Coast Guard has combined its Performance Report and Customer Service Report into a consolidated, corporate-style Coast Guard Annual Report. Here, the agency presents its performance goals, providing for each a discussion of actions taken to achieve results, major factors affecting strategies developed, and coordination with other organizations (including customers and stakeholders). In reporting the analysis and evaluation of the results, the annual report includes an illustration of the target, information for the past several years, and the trend line, as well as the initiatives defined as key by the Coast Guard.

Open communication, both internal and external, builds trust in the overall system, allows individuals and teams to shine, and restores faith in the capabilities of the organization.

CASE STUDY #1: INTERNAL REVENUE SERVICE

The Internal Revenue Service faces two major measurement challenges: (1) to translate the mission into measures that encourage desired performance, and (2) to design measures that balance customer service focus with overall tax administration responsibilities. At the IRS, the distinction between customer and client is clear.

The differences between previous approaches and the balanced approach now used at the IRS is reflected in the following table:

Previous	Balanced
Emphasis on achieving measures	Emphasis on achieving mission
Dependent on dollar results	Balanced priorities
No customer or employee measures	New customer satisfaction and employee satisfaction measures
Large number of measures	Small number of measures
Process measures used	Outcome measures used
Measures intended to address every situation	Measures allow for managerial judgment
Measures driven to front of organization	Measures aggregated from front of organization
Minimal attention to quality	Quality considered equally with quantity
Offices ranked	No ranking of offices

This new approach allows the IRS to understand both the taxpayer's and the employee's point of view while assessing and improving quality. As a result, the IRS has created an Office of Organizational Performance Management, which helps managers get closer to the work. Among the support activities for this are a tool kit for managers and multiple channels for feedback. The integrated operations plan and innovations are being given an opportunity to evolve in a less stressful environment, with temporary suspension of most reviews. The IRS realizes that organizational culture change takes time and that there are constraints on that evolution, including systems and data availability and a need for organizational learning.

Measuring Performance at the IRS

An integral part of the overall IRS modernization program is the establishment of a balanced measurement system that changes the way the service uses measures to assess progress against organizational goals, to identify improvement opportunities, and to plan for future challenges. As a result, the IRS has developed a set of balanced measures in three major areas: customer satisfaction, employee satisfaction, and business results. Each area represents an important aspect of the organization's goals and needs to be considered equally in taking action to carry out the service's programs and functions. This new approach to measurement advances principles outlined by the National Commission on Restructuring the IRS, the National Performance Review's Treasury/IRS Customer Service Task Force, and the Revenue and Restructuring Act of 1998, each of which advocated that the IRS balance its traditional focus on business results with measures of customer and employee satisfaction.

A critical aspect of building an appropriate balanced measurement system is establishing the measurements based on what an organization needs to achieve to advance its mission and strategic goals. In the past, the IRS used a number of quantity and productivity measures to report on its performance and justify its budget because those measures were easy to quantify and data was readily available. In an organization like the IRS, these measures consisted largely of enforcement statistics, especially enforcement revenue. Because "what gets measured is what gets done," the IRS managed and worked using this enforcement information, sometimes at the expense of other important considerations, such as customer and employee satisfaction.

In moving forward with the creation of a new organization focused on "providing America's taxpayers top quality service by helping them understand and meet their tax responsibilities and by applying the tax law with integrity and fairness to all," the IRS has changed what it uses to measure organizational performance. During the transition from the old organization to the new, modernized IRS, there was also a transition in measurements. The service began implementing the balanced measures in the areas of examination, collection, and customer service in January 1999. Work is now underway to apply the framework to other parts of the organization and to the new business units as they roll-out in FY 2000 and FY 2001.

The balanced measurement system at the IRS is very much a work in progress. For example, when a new measure has been developed, there needs to be at least one year of performance reporting to establish a baseline. The goal/target for the first year of the measure is therefore to establish a baseline. In some cases, information may be provided only biennially so that there is a two-year time lag between the establishment of the measure and the first targets set. At the same time, the organization's planning and review processes and the linking of measurements to various management practices are being redefined. Because the IRS is in the very early stages of implementing the balanced measurement approach, the measurements and the related processes will likely continue to be refined. However, the concept of what is being measured—customer satisfaction, employee satisfaction, and business results—will remain stable.

Establishing a Set of Measures

In developing the balanced measurement system, the IRS relied on the input and assistance of numerous individuals. Key IRS participants included national office and field executives, managers and staff at all levels, and frontline employees. Members of the National Treasury Employees Union (NTEU) were also included in the various working groups. Hundreds of IRS employees participated in interviews and focus groups and contributed in other ways to the development of the balanced measures system. These participants represented multiple functions and included representatives from service centers and districts. A steering committee composed of the Commissioner, the Deputy

Commissioner for Operations, the Treasury Assistant Secretary for Management/Chief Financial Officer, and the National President of NTEU met regularly to review progress and provide direction in the development of the system. In addition, input was received from external stakeholders in Congress, the Office of Management and Budget (OMB), and the Treasury. An outside consulting firm has provided assistance throughout the effort.

The IRS began the redesign of its performance measurement system in November 1997. The effort to develop and implement a balanced measurement approach began in earnest in April 1998. Rollout of the first components of the new measures began in January 1999. Application of the balanced measures framework across the organization and in the new business units will take several years.

The components of the balanced measurement system are aligned with the IRS strategic goals. The "service to each" goal, or customer satisfaction goal, is measured from the customer's point of view through the use of transactional surveys. The "service to all" goal, or business results goal, is measured by a combination of case or service quality and neutral quantities, such as number and mix of cases or services handled. The "productivity through a quality work environment" goal, or employee satisfaction goal, is measured by employee surveys of work environment satisfaction. When the balanced measures effort is fully implemented, the measures will be aligned with these strategic goals at all levels of the organization and will be composed of measures of customer satisfaction, employee satisfaction, and business results. To date, the focus of the balanced measures effort at the IRS has been on developing and implementing measures at the operational level. Activities at this level are presently carried out by "functions," such as customer service, examination, and collection. The development of measures at the strategic level for use in assessing progress toward achieving the overall mission and goals will take place once the new business units and organizational structure are in place. The new measures will be reviewed periodically to see if adjustments need to be made or if the related goals should be revised.

The IRS learned in 1997 that the measures it was using to encourage performance and to track outcomes were not balanced and could encourage inappropriate responses. Hearings focused on problem cases and testimony from employees who felt pressured to take enforcement actions to meet goals. To correct the weaknesses identified in the existing IRS measurement system, the commissioner established a task force in November 1997 to develop a new system of measures. The resulting new approach to measurement serves to advance principles outlined by the National Commission on Restructuring the IRS, the National Performance Review's Treasury/IRS Customer Service Task Force, and the Revenue and Restructuring Act of 1998, each of which advocated that the IRS balance its traditional focus on business results with measures of customer and employee satisfaction. Unlike previous measurement efforts, the redesigned measures will ensure that customer and employee satisfaction share equal importance with business results in driving the agency's actions and programs.

The balanced measurement system is composed of three categories of measures: customer satisfaction, employee satisfaction, and business results. These categories of measures are used because they align with the mission and will help in assessing organizational performance and progress toward the three qualitative organizational goals. As the service applies the balanced measures framework, organizational units will be required to develop measures in each category so that measures are aligned at all levels and the system is appropriately balanced.

Quantitative targets have been set only for those measures the service has used previously. Baselines are being established for the new measures that were introduced this year. Targets are set by the functional units who own the respective measures.

To measure employee satisfaction, the IRS will utilize information from an employee survey that will permit employees to provide an anonymous assessment of the wide variety of factors that determine whether they believe that the work environment permits them to perform their duties in a professional manner. Among other items included in the employee survey, the questionnaires will elicit information regarding employees' assessment of the quality of supervision and the adequacy of training and support services. Previous research has shown that employee perceptions are strongly linked to business results. Answers to the questions on the employee satisfaction survey will make up the employee satisfaction component of the balanced measurement system and will provide a gauge for assessing progress toward improving employee satisfaction.

In building this measure, employee feedback was collected about the previous Survey Feedback Action instruments in 1993, 1995, and 1997. The results? Employees felt there was a lack of accountability for elevated issues, a lack of clarity in questions, ineffective communication about positive actions taken, ineffective action planning above the workgroup, and questions not specific to levels of management. To address these concerns, the new employee satisfaction survey has been split into two parts: a work environment survey and a corporate survey. The work environment survey will be administered to address issues that are controllable at the workgroup or local management level. The corporate survey will gauge employee perception on broader organizational issues, covering topics such as quality/customer focus, resources/support/training, labor/management relations, management communications, ethics, trust/respect, and EEO/diversity. Results from the employee satisfaction work environment surveys will be used to identify improvement opportunities that will be incorporated into managerial performance plans and organizational work plans. The corporate survey results will feed into the organization's strategic plan.

The IRS has added an element of customer satisfaction to its performance measurement approach that will be used to identify service improvements and expectations from the customer's point of view.

To measure customer satisfaction, the IRS is collecting data from a statistically valid sample of taxpayers with whom it has dealt. Among other things, taxpayers are asked to provide information regarding whether they were treated courteously and professionally, whether they were informed of their rights, and whether they were given an opportunity to voice their concerns and adequate time to respond to IRS requests. Using data from these surveys, the IRS is deriving quantitative indices of customer satisfaction that will be used to measure progress toward improved customer satisfaction and to assess organizational performance, not individual performance.

A critical aspect of establishing an appropriate measurement system is basing the measurements on what the organization needs and wants to measure in order to achieve its strategic goals and mission, rather than simply on what is most easily measured. The measures should help tell employees how to support the mission. The IRS' balanced measurement system is designed to encourage employees to serve taxpayers professionally, to support an enabling work environment, to do quality work, and to work productively.

Efforts to develop balanced measures at the IRS are being coordinated through the Office of the Organizational Performance Management Executive. All organizational components are expected to develop a set of measures consistent with the balanced framework by utilizing measures of customer satisfaction, employee satisfaction, and business results.

Although it is still early in the process of implementing the new balanced approach to measurement, past experience has shown that success factors include: (1) ensuring that measures link to and support the desired behaviors expected of managers and employees, (2) establishing a clear link between the measures and the strategic goals and mission, and (3) having the top leadership committed to using the results to identify and execute improvement opportunities.

For several decades, the IRS has used statistics and measurements at all levels as part of its management process for the purpose of tracking how well organizational programs and services were working and to identify corrective actions as appropriate. In the past, enforcement statistics were a very key component of measuring performance at the IRS, both for internal management purposes and for justifying the IRS' overall budget to its stakeholders. However, the use of enforcement revenue as a measure of IRS performance created a dilemma and a controversy that persisted for years. The dilemma was created by the fact that each specific enforcement action must be guided by law as applied to the specific facts and circumstances of each case and, therefore, it has long been considered inappropriate to establish "quotas" or quantitative enforcement goals. Under the new balanced measurement system, enforcement dollars are not used as measures of performance. Instead, the new system balances measures of customer satisfaction, employee satisfaction, and business results.

Communication

The balanced measurement system was introduced to the organization using a variety of methods. First, two of the largest conferences in IRS history were convened to introduce executives, managers, and union leaders to the new measurement approach. Second, briefing sessions utilizing a highlights video from these conferences, a facilitator's guide, and a manager's communications tool kit are being conducted by heads of offices throughout the organization so that every employee and manager will know about and understand the changes taking place in how to measure organizational performance. Third, information about the measures redesign effort was regularly communicated throughout the organization using newsletters, voice messages, e-mails, and focus groups. Finally, a measures page was established on the IRS intranet, where a compendium of resources is available, a set of frequently asked questions is posted, and an e-mail address can be accessed to submit additional questions.

As part of the balanced measurement approach, the IRS is emphasizing the importance of "getting behind the numbers" to uncover the underlying causes or reasons for changes in performance. Traditionally, the IRS focused almost exclusively on meeting the numbers, and little consideration was given to the actions that were being taken to achieve the numbers and whether those were the right kinds of actions. To support this cultural change, the IRS is redesigning its review processes to ensure that they are aimed at identifying and discussing the factors that influence performance and not just at whether a number was met.

Establishing Accountability

The National Budget Office is responsible for preparing the servicewide strategic plan and the annual performance plan, which are developed utilizing input received from the various functional components of the IRS. Resource allocation plans are developed at all levels of the organization, but with increasing detail at lower levels. For example, broad resource allocations are made at the national level that are then translated into detailed allocation plans by the respective divisions or organizational units.

The IRS created the Office of Organizational Performance Management to formalize and centralize responsibility for coordinating all of the service's measurement efforts. The Organizational Performance Management Executive (OPME) has responsibility for reviewing and managing the service's use of performance information, including what data is collected, who has access to the data, and the purpose for which this data can be used (i.e., for program delivery, performance evaluation, or best practices discovery); ensuring the alignment of all agency planning and review processes with the principles of the balanced measurement system; assisting in the development, review, and refinement of measures; and reviewing all strategic documents and reports that contain measurement information prior to release.

Data collection, reporting, and posting of measurement results are the responsibility of the functions to which the measures are tied. For example, customer service is responsible for collecting data and reporting results about the IRS' toll-free services. Analysis of data has been a shared responsibility. The functions perform a significant amount of the analysis, but other parts of the organization, including the Research Office of Planning and Finance and the Office of Performance Evaluation and Risk Analysis, conduct additional analysis activities.

Measures ownership and accountability rest with the specific functions whose services and programs are being measured. Managers are held accountable for the performance of their work groups in meeting the goals and objectives outlined in the work plan. The measures provide an input for managerial assessment, but appraisals are based on managerial standards and consequently consider other factors. Individual employees are held accountable through critical elements and standards that are currently being updated to reflect more closely the service's new priorities as reflected in the balanced measures.

In determining accountability for specific performance results, the organization considers the impact of all those who have a role in contributing to that result through discussions aimed at uncovering the factors that influenced performance. At the highest levels, organizational goals are the shared responsibility of all executives and managers and are incorporated into performance plans and managerial standards.

In accordance with the Revenue and Restructuring Act of 1998, the IRS is currently redesigning its performance appraisal process. It has, however, been successful in linking accountability for results to performance measures. The problem has been ensuring that the measures are the right ones, that they serve to encourage the desired performance, and that the use of performance information for employees who have enforcement responsibilities does not violate legal statutes and policy restrictions.

Measuring Performance (Data Collection and Reporting)

The IRS uses a variety of systems to capture measurement data, which are identified in Appendix I of the IRS FY 2000 Budget Submission. The functional owners of the measures have responsibility for collecting the necessary data.

It is important to have a standard set of data requirements and a complete set of detailed information about each measure that includes the definition, the formula or methodology for calculating the measure, the frequency of data availability, the level of the organization to which results are available (i.e., national, district, branch, site), the data source, and the reliability or validity of the data collected.

The internal reporting and sharing of measurement results at the IRS is being reevaluated to ensure that the unintended negative consequences that resulted from previous approaches are not repeated.

The results of the IRS' measures are communicated to Congress through the Annual Program Performance Report, which is included with the budget submission. Results are also shared monthly with the Treasury Department, the Office of Management and Budget, and administration officials. In addition, the IRS regularly provides results to the General Accounting Office and the Treasury Inspector General for Tax Administration for use in carrying out their review and oversight responsibilities.

The IRS posts measurement results monthly to the Executive Management Support System (EMSS), which is accessible electronically to executives, managers, and analysts. There are restrictions on level of access. For example, managers are able to review results for their own site and higher levels of the organization but are restricted from reviewing results of other units.

Analyzing and Reviewing Performance Data

The IRS began to implement the balanced measurement system in 1999, and baseline data for most of the measures were collected during FY 2000. Additionally, the processes and organizational components responsible for analyzing and reviewing performance data are being reevaluated as part of the measures redesign effort and the modernization activities. As such, the IRS is unable to respond at this time to most of the questions in this section.

Analysis of measures data is done both internally by the IRS and by contractors. For example, the IRS uses contractors to administer the customer satisfaction and employee satisfaction surveys, and as part of their deliverables, the contractors provide detailed analyses of the survey results. The IRS performs additional analyses with the survey results, such as studying relationships between employee and customer satisfaction and business results.

The IRS has regularly reviewed its measures to ensure their continued relevance and usefulness and periodically established work groups servicewide or within specific functions to update or make revisions to the measures. They anticipate that this process will continue once the balanced measures are in place throughout the organization.

Evaluating, Using, and Reporting Performance Information to Customers and Stakeholders

The IRS uses performance information to assess progress toward organizational goals, to identify improvement opportunities, and to plan for future challenges. The plan is to use the various organizational review processes to identify opportunities for improving performance and to integrate the information into the organizational planning processes so that action plans for carrying out those improvements can be developed. It may be of interest to note that in the area of customer satisfaction, the IRS is using the results to initiate pilot tests to help validate and test the data and to learn how to improve customer satisfaction in a systematic way. The goal of these pilots is to determine the best way to integrate survey data into the way the IRS does business on a national and local level, thereby improving service to customers. The results will be used to develop guidelines and training for using survey data to identify best practices that can be shared with all offices.

The measured results serve as an input into appraisals; the focus, however, is on the actions that were taken to improve performance. Discussions and reviews are held to uncover the underlying causes of problems or issues and to identify actions that can be taken to resolve them. Those agreed-upon actions are included in performance plans and provide the basis for future reviews.

At the national level, the IRS conducts scheduled reviews of organizational performance at mid-year and at the end of the year. Performance reviews in the field occur more frequently. The IRS initiates additional reviews of performance when problems in service or program delivery become evident to uncover the causes of performance problems and to initiate corrective actions.

Under the new balanced measurement system, the measures are aligned with the IRS' strategic goals, which are in turn aligned with the mission. The measures will be used to assess progress toward achieving the goals.

The IRS met informally with representatives from public and private sector organizations that have balanced measurement systems in place or have begun developing such systems. These organizations included the National Security Agency, AT&T, Federal Express, and state tax agencies in Wisconsin, New York, and Kansas. In addition, the NPR IRS Customer Service Task Force conducted extensive benchmarking activities that led them to recommend that the IRS implement a balanced set of measures as a way to help improve service to taxpayers.

For further information, please contact Michael J. Novak at Mike.Novak@ccgate.irs.gov. The IRS's website is www.irs.ustreas.gov.

CASE STUDY #2: CITY OF CHARLOTTE, NORTH CAROLINA

The city of Charlotte began developing and implementing their balanced scorecard measurement system approximately three years ago. Charlotte's interest in the balanced scorecard approach resulted from its desire to use a more strategic, forward-looking framework to organize and implement performance measures. It had previously been measuring performance for decades in a more traditional management-by-objectives context.

In 1990, Charlotte City Council chose five areas (community safety, transportation, economic development, neighborhoods, and restructuring government) on which to focus its strategic plan. These priorities formed the basic categories in its "corporate" level scorecard. In the mid-1990s, several council members advocated for more outcome- or results-oriented measures. At about the same time, the city manager became interested in the balanced scorecard approach, having read Robert Kaplan and David Norton's early articles published in the *Harvard Business Review*. This essentially marked the beginning of the city's balanced scorecard efforts. During the first year of implementation in 1996, the city council established its "corporate" scorecard, and city staff from four pilot business units began developing their balanced scorecards. By the end of 1997, all 13 of the city's business units had at some level developed measures and balanced scorecards based on the corporate scorecard. Although Charlotte was the first U.S. city to adopt the balanced scorecard approach, the interviewee considered their work to be still evolving and maturing.

What the City Is Doing and Who Is Involved in the Process

Charlotte is pursuing a balanced scorecard approach to performance measurement in the more formal sense, that is, they categorize measures according to the four "perspectives" typically associated with a balanced scorecard: financial, customer, internal business processes, and learning and growth. All 13 of the city's business units participate in the measurement system, tracking a total of 266 measures. The customer perspective is the most emphasized of the four perspectives, accounting for 38% of the total measures. Internal processes account for 27%; growth and learning, 21%; and financial, 13%.

The next steps that Charlotte plans to take to improve its balanced scorecard system include the following: condensing the current list of performance measures to the "critical few," continuing to refine their business unit plans and scorecards, moving from the current semi-annual schedule to a quarterly reporting system, and eventually linking performance results and resource allocations.

How the City Is Using Balance Measures and Why It Is Valuable

Charlotte uses its balanced measures for several purposes: to communicate performance information to elected officials and the public, as input in its strategic planning process, in annual business unit and employee performance plans, and to identify areas for further evaluation and improvement.

The city of Charlotte's performance measurement effort has provided value to the city in the following ways:

- Measuring performance has clarified vague concepts like strategic goals.
- The balanced scorecard helped to integrate common goals across departments.
- It has allowed the city to set its performance measures into a more comprehensive, strategic context.
- It has encouraged the city to narrow its list of performance measures to those that are more meaningful and useful.
- Building the scorecards has developed consensus and teamwork throughout the organization.

The city identified the following five strategic themes using a balanced scorecard approach[7]:

1. Community safety
2. City within a city
3. Restructuring government
4. Transportation
5. Economic development.

The city's scorecard took into consideration the facets of the Kaplan/Norton Balanced Scorecard. (See Table 5-2.)

Lessons Learned

One of the key lessons learned has been that implementing a balanced scorecard system looks a lot easier than it is in reality. It requires city staff to learn new ways of thinking about the work they do and then to identify measures that gauge their success. This presents many challenges to management and staff related to changing existing practices. To meet these challenges and the expected resistance, management must remain committed to the effort over the long haul. It is also very helpful to have high-level champions who can provide committed leadership.

Another lesson learned was that challenging but achievable "stretch" targets must be set in a non-punitive context. If staff perceive that their budgets and other forms of support are at risk if actual performance results do not meet targets, buy-in and commitment will be negatively affected. Although Charlotte has begun to explore ways in which its balanced scorecard can be integrated into its resource allocation process, its is moving with care on this issue.

Potential Obstacles or Barriers and How Charlotte Dealt with Them

See above for a discussion of barriers regarding expected resistance, difficulty of this type of work, the premature linking of scorecard results and resource allocations, and how Charlotte has dealt with these issues.

For further information, please contact: Lisa Schumacher, Budget Officer, at bulbs@mail.charmeck.nc.us. The city's website is www.ci.charlotte.nc.us/cimanager/about1.htm.

Table 5-2
City of Charlotte's Scorecard

Charlotte's Goals and Objectives

BSC Categories							
Customer Perspective	Reduce Crime	Increase Perception of Safety	Strengthen Neighborhoods	Improve Service Quality	Make Safe, Convenient Transportation Available	Maintain Competitive Tax Rates	Promote Economic Opportunity
Financial Accountability			Expand Non-City Funding	Maximize Benefit-Cost Ratio	Grow Tax Base	Maintain AAA Rating	
Internal process	Increase positive contacts	Promote Community-Based Problem Solving	Secure Funding/Service Partners	Improve Productivity	Streamline Customer Interactions	Increase Infrastructure Capacity	Promote Business Mix
Learning & Growth			Enhance Knowledge Management Capabilities	Close Skills Gap	Achieve Positive Employee Climate		

CASE STUDY #3: COMMONWEALTH OF VIRGINIA

The Commonwealth of Virginia has been implementing a fully integrated performance management strategy since the early 1990s. Virginia's performance budgeting process represents a major evolution in the state's past efforts in strategic planning and performance measurement by fully integrating strategic planning and performance measurement with agency and program budgeting. By integrating these three elements into a single process, Virginia has been able to link agency mission, program priorities, anticipated results, strategies for achieving results, and budgeting.

For Virginia, this performance budgeting process enhances the state's financial management in three areas:

- Accountability for program outcomes where outcome measures are linked to program goals
- Long-term focus that links daily operations to the key strategies identified in each agency strategic plan
- Prioritization of resources that will result from being able to base budget decisions on the results to be achieved rather than on traditional baseline budgeting.

The performance budgeting process is designed to focus on customers and results. Each agency is required to identify the customers that are served by each service, program, or process, and then to assess the expectations of those customers. Agency strategic plans are based on this customer analysis, and resources are allocated to achieve the desired results.

Virginia's performance budgeting process begins with a comprehensive strategic assessment in which each state agency analyzes its state and federal mandates, customers and customer service, agency mission and activities, organizational strengths, weaknesses, threats, opportunities, and critical issues facing the agency. Based on these analyses, each agency then develops strategies, goals, and objectives that constitute the agency strategic plan.

State agencies use these strategic plans to develop activity-based budgets and performance measures. Each agency develops and submits several performance measures that relate to its highest priority activities. At least one measure is required to be an outcome measure focused on broad program results. Performance measures were published in 1996 along with baseline date and established targets. Progress toward each measure is reported to the public each December with the governor's budget document, and this information is available on the Department of Planning and Budgets' Website.

The budget document includes actual agency performance at the end of the fiscal year for selected measures (three to five for most agencies and six core measures for each institution of higher education). Of the 684 performance measures for agencies, there are 507 outcome measures, 91 output measures, 53 efficiency measures, and 33 input measures.

- Outcome measures indicate the extent to which an activity or program has met stated objectives, such as percent reduction in recidivism or parts per million of specific airborne pollutants.
- Output measures indicate the amount of work accomplished by a program or activity, such as the number of clients served.
- Efficiency measures generally express a resource utilized per unit of output, such as cost per lane mile paved or staff hours expended per case.
- Input measures indicate the resources that are invested in a program or activity, such as total dollars appropriated or staff hours expended.

Performance measures provide an invaluable internal management for agencies to monitor program performance and take corrective action for improving service to customers.

Virginia continues to expand the use of performance measures. In 1999, the governor completed a statewide strategic plan that will link agency plans and budgets more closely to his agenda. In addition, Virginia is also investigating the development of a set of societal measures to link performance to broader state circumstances.

Currently, Virginia's performance budgeting process is best described as a very sophisticated and effective activity-based performance budgeting system rather than a scorecard of balanced measures. However, the development of the governor's strategic plan and the growing interest in identifying societal measures is raising both the strategic vision and organizational alignment issues that the balanced scorecard model has evolved to address.

As activity-based management and balanced measures approaches continue to evolve, Virginia's performance budgeting process clearly represents a benchmark for any state that is interested in improving results and accountability.

For further information, please contact Herb Hill, Director of Strategic Planning, Research and Evaluation, Virginia Department of Planning/Budget, Hhill@dpb.state.va.us. The state's website is www.state.va.us/dpb.

CHAPTER 6

Leading the Public Sector Organization in a Changing World

- Sharing the Leadership Role
- The Leader as Educator
- The Leader as Architect
- The Leader as Caretaker
- Establishing Strong Performance Management Principles

> A boss creates fear; a leader, confidence. A boss fixes blame; a leader corrects mistakes. A boss knows all; a leader asks questions. A boss makes work drudgery; a leader makes it interesting. A boss is interested in him or herself; a leader is interested in the group.
>
> —Russell H. Ewing

Leadership does not—and cannot—stop at the top, but must cascade throughout an organization, creating champions and a team approach to achievement of the mission. Leadership by employees in solving problems and achieving the mission is what makes for a most successful organization. As a leader of innovation in the public sector, you need to know the expectations of your stakeholders and the client, whether as a recipient of the benefit or service or as a taxpayer. What does the employee need to meet those expectations? Goals and objectives cannot be achieved without taking those expectations and needs into account. Most important, cascading leadership creates an environment in which each individual employee is aware of his or her role in the achievement of the departmental mission. A public sector organization that has achieved this cultural change will have a sustainability that becomes ingrained in the fabric of the organization.

The challenge to management is to use flexibility to pro-vide a solution to problems. Individuals may be rewarded for their achievements by being promoted into management level positions. To become good managers, however, they need training in human resource issues. Managers must take responsibility for poor performers, think in terms of partnering, and use available tools to present information for analysis clearly and efficiently.

Leadership is a critical element marking successful organi-zations, both public and private. Cascaded throughout an organization, leadership gives the performance manage-ment process a depth and sustainability that survives changes at the top—even those driven by elections and changes in political party leadership.

> The Vice President for Strategic Planning is the process owner for strategic planning at the U.S. Postal Service. The USPS strategic plan looks out over a period of five years and endeavors to understand and position USPS for what the "voices" will be saying in five years' time. The mission is linked to the "voices" as indicated by performance trends. USPS does not issue an annual strategic plan; rather, it issues a new strategic plan every couple of years, depending on the need for course corrections.

Two experts in the field, the Honorable Maurice McTigue, a former New Zealand cabinet member now working at George Mason University, and Patricia Ingraham, Ph.D., of the Maxwell School at Syracuse University, emphasize in their teaching the importance of leadership in a political environment. Given the potential constraints such an envi-ronment can present, a successful public sector organization needs strong leadership that supports the adoption of bal-anced measures as a feature of organizational management and accountability.

> At the Veterans Benefits Administration, the current Under Secretary for Benefits, Joe Thompson, provides strong leader-ship to the process. He had a positive experience with a bal-

anced set of measures at the VBA's New York office and felt strongly about applying this approach to the entire organization. His leadership has been the driving force behind the application of a BSC approach at the VBA.

A balanced set of measures allows leaders to think of their organization in its totality. There is no one "right" family of measures. The measures must reflect the overall mission and strategy of the organization. They have to drive the organization in its day-to-day activities. In most cases, they are developed through an iterative, evolutionary process. You can have as many categories as you want, but you should keep it as simple as possible so that your measurements can be global and quick.

There is no generic set of balanced measures that can be applied as best practice to all functions of the public sector. Certain conditions, however, need to exist within any public sector organization for a balanced approach to performance management to be successful:

- Strong leadership that supports the adoption of balanced measures as a feature of organizational management and accountability
- The capability to communicate effectively throughout the organization and the organization's ability to communicate to decision makers
- The knowledge that customers, employees, and stakeholders are fully informed and that they understand and support the initiatives of the organization.

The city of Charlotte, North Carolina, found that implementing a balanced set of measures system is much more difficult than it had at first expected. It also learned the importance of developing challenging but achievable stretch targets and placing them in a non-punitive context. Leaders recognized that buy-in and commitment from employees is compromised if the system is initially structured to put budgets at risk if a performance target is not met. During the initial phases of culture change, they found it was best to leave the employees with some breathing room—to let them know that they and the city organization are struggling through this together rather than that this was some sort of "us versus them" situation.

SHARING THE LEADERSHIP ROLE

Without exception, successful organizations, both public and private, cite strong leadership as a key factor in their success in applying a balanced approach to performance management. Without support from senior management and top officials, it is difficult, although not impossible, to establish a successful strategic framework that integrates all the necessary factors.

U.S. Coast Guard Commandant James Loy has made performance measurement an imperative of his tenure. He requires his service to use quantitative performance data in the stewardship and management of its resources to provide the "greatest public good."

Certain leadership truisms apply whether an organization's management structure is a pyramid, like Canada's St. Lawrence Seaway Management Corporation, or more like a web, characterized by interconnections crisscrossing throughout the structure. These truisms include:

(1) Good leadership relies on good communication.
(2) All members of the organization must have clearly defined responsibilities.

The best leaders report back to the employees, customers, and other stakeholders; use self-assessment tools, such as the Baldrige criteria; involve the legislative branch through consultation or representation on working groups and committees; involve the customer, stakeholder, and employee at every phase of the management process; and involve the unions early and often.

Two of the more significant lessons learned concern the decentralization of Phoenix's approach and the frequency with which data can be used. The city's first foray into performance measurement was characterized by a relatively top-down, centralized approach that included mandates on how to define measures and, in some cases, which measures to use. City management quickly encountered stiff resistance to this approach and has since pursued the more flexible, department-driven approach described above. Asking departmental managers to use only those measures they perceive to be functional in their particular context has facilitated both citywide buy-in and the use of more relevant measures. According to the interviewee, had the city not shifted its approach and continued with a top-down strategy, it would likely have had little success with performance measurement.

The stereotypical "great leader" in our culture is the rugged individual, carving out a role and marching forward, the troops following faithfully (and blindly) behind. Unfortunately, this type of individual traditionally would focus on a short-term result rather than long-term goals and objectives.

Today's public sector organizations face relatively new concepts of strategic planning and accountability for the achievement of their missions. These responsibilities require a very different type of leader—one who can build an organizational consciousness. The "new" organization shares a common vision of the future, and individual employees work together to achieve that vision.

This process creates a natural tension between where the organization currently is and where it wants to be. Peter M. Senge, Director of the Systems Thinking and Organizational Learning program at the MIT Sloan School of Management, likens this tension to a rubber band stretched between two hands. The lower of the two hands is where the organization currently is, and the upper hand is where it wants to be. To relieve the stress, either the reality has to be raised or the expectations lowered.

Today's leader must create that tension, which requires three distinct efforts. First, there has to an accurate evaluation of the current status of the organization. This means a "reality check," perhaps based in a SWOT analysis (see Chapter 3). To create an accurate picture, there needs to be feedback from everyone: customer and client (not always the same people), stakeholder, and employee. Second, a vision of the future has to be developed in consonance with the views of the same groups of individuals. The third element—communicating the first two elements throughout the organization—is the most vital and perhaps the most challenging.

This type of leadership allows individuals to move toward the goal, armed with a knowledge of the two ends of the spectrum. Unlike the traditional problem-solving methods, it does not wait for a crisis to react. It is a proactive, rather than reactive, method of development.

The roles of today's leader in the above process are three-fold: educator, architect, and caretaker.

THE LEADER AS EDUCATOR

As an educator, today's leader helps every individual understand both the current reality and the vision for the future. As the vision is evolving through discussions with stakeholders, customers, and employees, there should be an awareness of training or system changes that will be needed to achieve the future vision. What training does the individual employee need to do his or her job better? Do the organization's data systems provide accurate information in a timely manner so that the employee can make a well-informed decision? To achieve an organizational mission, the organization must be able to act in a unified manner. What is being done in your organization to cross-train individuals from different perspectives? Is your organization "stove-piped"? Remember that individual employees cannot fully comprehend their roles in the overall process unless and until they understand the process itself!

Education is also a vital part of the communication effort. Not only the employees need to know and understand individual roles and responsibilities—customers, clients, and stakeholders also need to be able to see "the big picture" and understand the challenges the organization may be facing in trying to achieve its mission. The role of the leader as educator in this phase is one of communicator. Stakeholders especially want to understand the challenges, and employees will look to the leader of the organization to see how they respond to questions. If the leader of the organization does not accept responsibility, then the employee will certainly be less likely to do so. Lead by example.

THE LEADER AS ARCHITECT

For the organization to achieve a stated mission or vision, it must have a road map showing how to get from here to there. Earlier in this book, there was a discussion of viewing the approach as being like the flight panel on an airplane or the dashboard of a car. The same metaphors apply here. The airline may want the airplane to go at specific speeds and maintain certain rates of efficiency, but if the person who built the plane didn't do the job correctly, all the flight plans in the world will not make that plane capable. Alternatively, even though the speed limit is 65 for many interstate roads and the driver of the car may want to reach a destination at a specific time, a car that was not designed correctly won't make it there on time.

Regardless of which metaphor you choose, a balanced approach allows you to consider all the important operational measures at the same time, letting you see whether improvement in one area is achieved at the expense of another. Key indicators should tell you how the organization is doing. They can change over time to reflect a shifting in emphasis for organizational goals. Performance levels can be reported on a monthly or quarterly basis. All levels of management, including field personnel, can participate in the reporting process; together, they provide a good idea of the health of the organization from a variety of perspectives. It is only with a balanced approach that leaders can create success throughout their organizations.

This proven approach to strategic management imbeds long-term strategy into the management system through the mechanism of measurement, translating vision and strategy into a tool that effectively communicates strategic intent and motivates and tracks performance against established goals.

The architect of today's organization must establish the vision and core values by which the organization will function. Those concepts then translate into strategies that in turn determine day-to-day policy decisions. The architect cannot design this structure in a vacuum. If you were designing a house, you would consult with the people who will live in the house. By the same token, today's leader must involve customers, clients, stakeholders, and employees in the creation of a mission-oriented organization, focused on a unified vision for the future.

> In the city of Phoenix, the regular measuring of performance has created and supported a work environment in which improvement and results are important. While performance data cannot always be tied directly to innovation and improvement efforts, this general environment is consistent with one of Phoenix's core values—a focus on results.

THE LEADER AS CARETAKER

Senge refers to this role as the "servant leader," a term also used by Robert Greenleaf in his book *Servant Leadership: A Journey into the Nature of Legitimate Power and Greatness* (New York: Paulist Press, 1977). Greenleaf states: "The servant leader is servant first . . . This conscious choice brings one to aspire to lead."

Today's leader must tend to the employees, the organization itself, its vision, mission, and goals. When an organization is undergoing reinvention, people are uncertain about their role in the "new" organization and, sometimes, whether their jobs are secure. In many cases, especially in the public sector, the concepts of accountability and responsibility are being redefined. Being held accountable for measures that may not be totally under an individual's control can cause anxiety. A leader needs to be aware of that potential for anxiety and use open lines of communication to assuage those fears.

Leadership that takes into account feedback from its employees, customers, and stakeholders, together with performance data, has a full scope of information upon which to make informed decisions. And it is a basic tenet of good management that the more informed the decision, the sounder that decision will be.

It verges on paradoxical that a good leader must be a catalyst who institutes a culture that will survive changes in leadership and administration. The key here is to cascade leadership throughout an organization and to give ownership of strategic plans and performance measures to career employees. That ownership, which involves organizational learning and culture change, is necessary for sustainability.

> "You change culture by changing the conversation. The theory behind reinvention is that you must change the way people do their job in order to change the culture. At the same time, you must continually think about how this will be accomplished, while at the same time serving your customers."
> —Morley Winograd, Senior Policy Advisor to Vice President Al Gore and Director of the National Partnership for Reinventing Government

ESTABLISHING STRONG PERFORMANCE MANAGEMENT PRINCIPLES

- Expect excellence
- Establish accountability
- Take timely action.

Expect Excellence

Federal managers should establish a set of balanced measures and communicate those expectations to the individual employee. The objective of this effort is to ensure that employees have a clear idea of what is expected of them. Feedback should be ongoing, rather than the once or twice a year that evaluations are scheduled. This type of open communication also serves to alleviate some of the anxiety referred to above because the leader becomes a caretaker by constant feedback and communication.

Establish Accountability

Managers should be measured on how well they meet their responsibilities as leaders. Do managers focus rewards on real results? Are managers trained to be managers? This concept is quite new to the public sector. Individuals are traditionally promoted to positions of leadership within a division or program because they are good at their jobs. There is an innate fallacy here in that simply because an individual is good at a job (e.g., accounting or engineering), it does *not* mean that they will automatically be good managers!

To become a good manager requires training, and an organization that wants to achieve success has to be willing to spend the time and money to train their managers. "People skills" need to be developed, including how to establish and maintain an open line of communication and how to appraise performance. Good managers are not born; skills are developed through training and experience, neither of which stands alone.

Take Timely Action

Poor performance should be addressed early: Do not wait until it makes an impact on the organization. Early intervention, including training, counseling, and open communication, can prevent poor performance from becoming a major problem. Sharing best practices can also help. Rather than merely telling someone that they are doing something wrong, suggest that they try another approach that has been successful elsewhere.

The PMC plan asks agencies to draft performance agreements with the highest levels of departmental leadership for the next appraisal cycle. Those agreements would contain a balanced set of performance measures, dealing with customer satisfaction, employee involvement, and success in performance planning.

If the leadership of a public sector organization works, it will result in internal and external support for organizational initiatives. Internally, ownership will be given to the employees, allowing each one to be a leader within his or her own sphere. For example, the Canadian St. Lawrence Seaway Management Corporation organizes its performance indicators according to a clearly delineated pyramid. All employees know where they fit into the structure and what they are expected to achieve.

Top-level support in successfully establishing a balanced set of measures can be seen in numerous organizations where this strong executive leadership has cascaded throughout the organization.

The Internal Revenue Service has worked diligently over the past year to establish a balanced set of measures; its dedication to creating such a performance measurement system stems directly from its commissioner, Charles O. Rossotti. Commissioner Rossotti made a commitment to redirect the IRS's focus from internal processes to the customer, and major strides have been made in this direction.

Performance-based management has been a major part of the successful organizational changes led by Dr. Kenneth Kizer, Under Secretary for Health at the Department of Veterans Affairs (1994–1999). His leadership resulted in a sustainable process that has continued beyond his term of service.

> The wicked leader is he whom the people despise.
> The good leader is he whom the people revere.
> The great leader is he whom the people say, "We did it ourselves."
>
> —Lao Tsu

CASE STUDY #1: VETERANS BENEFITS ADMINISTRATION

The Department of Veterans' Affairs is composed of three organizational elements: (1) the Veterans' Health Administration, (2) the National Cemetery Administration, and (3) the Veterans' Benefits Administration. The Veterans Benefits Administration deals with housing, insurance, compensation, pension, education, vocational rehabilitation, and counseling for veterans. The compensation area takes care of monthly payments to veterans for disabilities related to military service and to dependents in event of a veteran's death. The pension area addresses monthly payments to veterans or surviving dependents. Educational benefits are for service members and veterans after separation from service, as well as active reservists. Vocational Rehabilitation and Counseling rehabilitation services help disabled veterans obtain and keep employment or severely disabled veterans to gain a level of independence in their daily living. Housing at the VBA helps veterans with credit assistance in becoming homeowners, and insurance provides life insurance for service members and veterans. Nationally, there are 57 regional offices, with nine service delivery networks (SDNs) to accomplish the mission and goals recently created.

> ***Balanced Scorecard:*** This is an organizational tool that translates an organization's mission strategy into objectives and measures organized into four different perspectives: financial, customer, internal business process, and learning and growth. It provides all employees with information they can use to effect the results the organization is achieving.
> —Glossary of Terms, *The Balanced Scorecard Handbook*, VBA, October 1998

Establishing a Balanced Set of Measures

In 1980s–90s, the Philadelphia office started actively using TQM. Joe Thompson, who now leads the VBA as the Under Secretary for Benefits, was involved in the process there. He later moved to the New York office, where GPRA brought about the balanced scorecard concept. In that office, they expanded stakeholder involvement beyond OMB and Congress to include veterans and taxpayers.

The New York office became an NPR Reinvention Lab. As a result, that office provided the skeleton of key measures that the VBA modified and now uses. These key measures are speed, accuracy, cost, customer satisfaction, and employee development. The BSC, as an approach nationwide by the VBA, began as part of the efforts to comply with the Government Performance and Results Act of 1993. Senior officials, staff managers, line managers, customers (indirectly), stakeholders, employees, labor partnerships, and contractors were all involved in developing the BSC.

A committee was formed from Regional Office and Central Office senior managers. Their initial goal was to ensure that compliance with GPRA was not merely a bureaucratic exercise but rather the establishment of a process that would be beneficial to the VBA as a whole. The performance measures that they defined were measures that would have meaning across all their business lines. The BSC provided the framework for this, and the committee did process mapping—defining what every business line does, exactly how they do it, and identifying performance gaps. This steering committee developed business plans for each one of the business lines and began integrating the budget into these plans. Thompson, who had been a member of the original committee representing the New York regional office, became the Under Secretary at the VBA and helped develop a road map for change.

In December of 1997, Thompson conducted a series of planning sessions. Prior to this, the measures used were internal and did not take into account customer satisfaction. In January of 1998, the *Road Map to Excellence* was developed and a BSC Team formed. In June of that year, the Data Management Office was formed. Its role is to provide a centralized location for data warehousing. (See the section on flexibility under "Lessons Learned" below.)

In April 1999, the VBA published an electronic BSC on its intranet. Thompson views this step as one of the first steps in an iterative process designed to improve performance. The VBA has a balanced scorecard consistent with the basic framework of Kaplan and Norton. Although some of the measures are still in development, the VBA has the four basic categories of measures: financial (unit cost), internal (timeliness and accuracy), customer satisfaction and learning, and growth (employee development).

Measuring Performance—Data Collection and Reporting

The performance information used to be e-mailed to the field offices, but the VBA began to use the intranet in November 1998, ensuring that everyone has access to a consistent set of information. The SDNs use the intranet and the performance information on the balanced scorecard for day-to-day management decisions. They do not, however, use the performance information on the intranet as a grading tool. Source data for each measure is included on the site, and the data is very visible and available to all employees.

Currently, data warehouse technology is used to gather data and generate the balanced scorecard and supporting reports. This feature was enhanced to allow users to query directly against the data warehouse to generate *ad hoc* queries and reports.

Although the general public does not see the VBA balanced scorecard, it is available to employees, and the measures are available to the general public through the departmental annual performance plan.

Analyzing and Reviewing Performance Data

The Data Management Office (DMO) is responsible for collecting and compiling the data and for producing and publishing the balanced scorecard. The DMO, business lines, and Office of Field Operations work in partnership to analyze the data. (See also the discussion on flexibility under "Lessons Learned.")

Evaluating, Using, and Reporting Performance Information to Customers and Stakeholders

FY 1999 was the first year the BSC was used, and it was a major transition within the VBA. Offices track the BSC at their level (service delivery networks, regional offices, and divisions in regional offices), and some tracking is also done at the team level. Every six weeks to two months, VBA leadership meets to review the BSC at each level (national, regional, and service delivery networks). SDNs meet at least quarterly to discuss their performance.

The VBA holds BSC "summits" for mid-term review and input from the field stations. The issues and proposed solutions gathered from this summit are aggregated by the DMO into four areas:

1. Administrative issues
2. Field issues/concerns
3. Service/business line issues/concerns
4. Completing the "to be determined" items on the balanced scorecards.

> "Communication is critical to the process throughout—from its inception, when you make the decision to create a scorecard, to the point in time where it is produced. You must have an open, honest dialogue regarding what it takes to get the job done."
> —Chuck DeCoste, director of the VBA's Data Management Office

Links Between the Strategic Plan and Resource Allocation

Each of the balanced scorecard strategic objectives is contained in the business line plans, which the VBA has integrated with its budget submission. All scorecard measures are therefore linked to resource requests. The linking of resources directly with the performance objectives in a balanced approach is a significant challenge. It requires a mature process and experience with the scorecard and performance budgeting in order to form a direct link between scorecard performance and resources. This is not an issue unique to the VBA but indeed is important throughout the public sector.

Benchmarking

Because the VBA is very similar to a commercial company, it benchmarked with similar insurance companies and organizations in several areas, e.g., telephone times and money to beneficiaries (disbursements). They also use some NPR-suggested benchmarks for standards. The VBA is developing a website to share best practices.

Lessons Learned

Two factors were instrumental for the VBA in implementing the BSC: flexibility and communication. The structure of the BSC, like all strategic planning processes, is iterative, and the established process must be flexible enough to work not only for headquarters but also for the field offices, while simultaneously allowing for comparisons among offices. The Data Management Office makes the national data easily accessible for both national use and further analysis. The consistency that results from this type of warehousing results in every employee seeing the same information. Another facet of flexibility at the VBA is that measures are universal, but the weight given to each measure may differ among business lines. The BSC provides the framework, but there is flexibility within that framework to make it work for the individual organization.

The VBA found that communication, both internal and external, was also critical to the success of the BSC. Employees need to know where they fit into the process, and customers and stakeholders can use the BSC approach to understand the goals and processes of the organization. Communication is also used to build consensus within the organization as to what was to be measured and reported. Initial analysis of what had been measured historically at the VBA showed that the old systems did not measure the three most important groups: veterans, employees, and taxpayers. The employee development measures were the most difficult to develop. The unions were involved in developing them; they always have an interest in education issues for employees. In the education program area, they may have the first fully-developed employee measure in a skills matrix in New York that the VBA now uses as a model for development for all VBA employees. The score for employee development is determined by the number of employees who have the skills the organization needs to deliver service. The VA conducted a department-wide employee survey in 1997 and an internal survey for employees during FY 1999. The department-wide survey data serves as a baseline. The education program's measures were more natural and easy to develop.

Other lessons learned as a result of the BSC process discussed include:

1. The customer demands measuring performance.
2. The BSC allows better measurement against private industry.
3. The BSC leads to more collaboration in the whole organization.
4. The BSC forces a more holistic view of work.
5. The BSC provides a clear message to the field from headquarters.
6. The BSC allows easy view of your progress.
7. Most important, strong senior leadership is key to the development of the BSC in an organization.

For further information, please contact Dennis Thomas at ormdthom@vba.va.gov. The VBA's website is www.vba.va.gov.

CASE STUDY #2: ST. LAWRENCE SEAWAY MANAGEMENT CORPORATION

> Measure the right things and measure them right.
> —Carmen Nadeau, Performance Management
> Coordinator, St. Lawrence Seaway Management
> Corporation

The St. Lawrence Seaway Management Corporation (SLSMC) is a Canadian not-for-profit organization responsible for the safe and efficient movement of marine traffic through Canadian seaway facilities. SLSMC is the former SLSA (The St. Lawrence Seaway Authority—Crown corporation), of which most operations were commercialized (as of October 1998) to a nine-member mixed user/government board accountable to Parliament through the Minister of Transport. SLSMC is essentially financially self-sufficient. A five-year business plan defines expectations of the board and minister. The U.S. St. Lawrence Seaway District Commission is responsible for the U.S. portion of the St. Lawrence Seaway and is a partner in operations and marketing. A small consultant firm helped them develop a measurement method based on the balanced scorecard approach.

Establishing/Updating Performance Measures and Goals

Senior management established an eight-person team in March 1995 with the goals of identifying seaway activities that are key to success of the organization (key success factors) and designing a measurement system. Key indicator categories and associated indicators were based on:

- The mission statement from its own Authority Act (what the American public sector commonly refers to as "enacting language")

- The vision statement
- The corporate objectives.

A five-person team was put in place in January 1996 to oversee implementation. Measures were developed based on extensive consultation within and outside the organization. Some 24 indicators were developed as a result of this consultation and other mechanisms. The indicators are currently being adjusted to reflect change to a new, more commercialized not-for-profit setup. Defining factors included:

- A need to trigger action (can you take action to improve the performance of activity measured?)
- A proper balance in consultation with stakeholders, customers, employees, and the government as owner of waterway
- Clear links to corporate/strategic objectives and key success factors
- Integration of measures between organizational levels (pyramid approach—see Accountability and Reporting) and individual jobs.

The measures were also expected to take into account the interrelationship between indicators (e.g., reliability and cost indicators, or finding the balance to spending more money on infrastructure while maintaining cost effectiveness).

Mission, vision, and objectives have all been restated to align with the new, more commercialized not-for-profit setup. There are five new strategic objectives (each with strategies and projects):

- Meet and exceed business plan expectation
- Increase customer satisfaction
- Increase infrastructure reliability
- Increase competitiveness
- Increase employee satisfaction.

A performance measurement system must be a living item.

Establishing Accountability for Performance

Carmen Nadeau is responsible for coordination and maintenance of the performance measurement system, including coordination of data collection. Data analysis is left to the employees or teams, who actually own the performance measurement system. (The team concept was introduced to the organization about the same time as the measurement system.)

SLSMC is exploring linking individual performance to that of the seaway. The measurement system is currently disassociated from individual performance evaluations to promote objective performance reporting. There is widespread acceptance that change in culture is required before moving to individual accountability.

SLSMC has a pyramid approach, empowering all levels from executive to operational (see Figure 6-1):

- Level One—executive management team
    - looks at long-term, global trends and summary reports
    - concerned with overall strategy
- Level Two—vice presidents and management team
    - look at specific trends and regional and local reports
    - concerned with planning and some monitoring
- Level Three—manager and supervisor teams
    - look at regional and local reports
    - concerned with monitoring and some planning
- Level Four—frontline teams
    - look at details and fast response time
    - concerned with problem-solving and improvements

The measurement system was transferred to the intranet in 1998 and access opened to all. However, each team has its own "dashboard" (control panel that provides the indicators relevant to the team, i.e., those the team can act on). Data is tailored to their area of responsibility and provided at the frequency relevant to their level on the pyramid (e.g., most indicators are annual at Level 1, as their perspective is more strategic than operational; frequency increases as we move down the pyramid).

Figure 6-1
SLSMC Pyramid

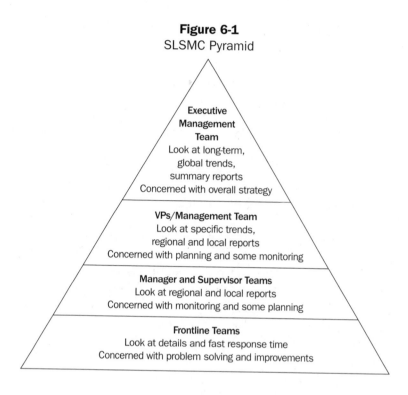

New strategic objectives cascade down the organization and "translate" to specific targets at each level where relevant.

The company newsletter reports on the implementation of the performance measurements. There is a commitment to an educational process to show that using performance measurement is a self-improvement tool. Reporting on the status and results of measurements is done at team meetings within the SLSMC internal management process.

Measuring Performance (Data Collection and Reporting)

SLSMC uses an Oracle database with feeder systems. Information is gathered mainly at Levels 3 and 4 of the pyramid.

Lessons learned regarding managing a large amount of data:

- They may not have researched thoroughly enough what package to use; the Oracle graphics package is cumbersome to update when upgrades to indicators are required.
- There was an assumption that training one level would result in ownership and training of the next level. Cascading results were long to achieve.

Analyzing and Reviewing Performance Data

To encourage utilization of the measurement system, senior management analyzed one indicator monthly. This began the process because other levels had to answer. SLSMC now has Level 1 owners for each key processes within the organization and associated indicators. Owners will be identified for other levels when new strategic objectives are cascaded down the organization.

At Levels 3–4, indicators show measures that affect the operations area. When employees or teams analyze performance, there could be three reasons why the indicators are not up to par:

(1) Data may be incorrect (data input)
(2) Measurement system could be wrong (indicator design)
(3) Process being measured needs improvement.

Process improvement is at the heart of performance measurement. Improvement teams are put in place to correct any process deficiencies identified.

Evaluating, Using, and Reporting Performance Information to Customers and Stakeholders

Customer consultation has played an important role in the development of customer-related indicators. By agreement with users, certain types of delays (e.g., fog) are not included to calculate transit time achievement. Transit time targets of 90% transit within norm + 2 hours and 95% transit within norm + 4 hours were defined with the customers. Results and targets are reviewed with customers yearly and adjusted if required. A new customer survey will be designed by year 2000 to better evaluate overall customer satisfaction.

Reliability indicator data are used for asset renewal justifications, providing some linking to budget. New cost, FTE (full time equivalents), and asset renewal indicators are being developed to monitor business plan achievement. Indicators are also used in reporting to the Board of Directors on key processes.

Users and general public have access to summarized information through the annual report.

Links Between Strategic Plan and Resource Allocation

Indicator results were used in strategic planning exercise to assess strengths and weaknesses as well as opportunities and threats. Performance measurement influences market strategy product and service design and operational strategies. As indicated above, reliability indicator data are used for budget justifications, and new cost indicators will monitor business plan achievement.

Each of the five strategic objectives has an indicator associated to it with specific targets. Resource allocation within the strategic plan was done to support achievement of strategic objectives as measured by indicators.

Best Practices

Performance measures are:

- Able to be put into action
- Linked to mission/vision
- Balanced
- Integrated
- Owned by employees.

SLSMC avoided creating another layer to collect data because results will not find an owner.

Benchmarking

SLSMC currently conducts employee satisfaction surveys every two years to determine:

- Overall satisfaction
- How aligned they are with vision and objectives.

SLSMC is benchmarking employee satisfaction and alignment using the databank from Hay Consulting Group. This is a databank of companies that have done employee surveys.

SLSMC is still trying to benchmark vessel integrity (number of accidents to vessels through systems, although finding comparable data has proven difficult. They will benchmark against competing systems, beginning this summer. Finally, attempts have also been made to benchmark lost time injury data.

For further information, please contact Carmen Nadeau, Performance Management Coordinator, Voice Mail: (613) 932-5170 extension 3258, E-mail: cnadeau@seaway.ca.

CASE STUDY #3: FLORIDA DEPARTMENT OF ENVIRONMENTAL PROTECTION

The Program Administrator for Strategic Projects and Planning gave a thorough and enthusiastic presentation about the results-based performance measurement/management system of the agency.

For the past several years, the growth in environmentally regulated entities has greatly exceeded the growth of their budgets. In addition, the impacts that are having the largest effect on the environment have broadened to include unregulated impacts, such as non-point source runoff. As a result, it is becoming increasingly difficult for environmental agencies to make gains using strictly traditional approaches.

In response, the FDEP began to focus and manage for results by building a performance measurement system that identifies emerging problems and supplies the contextual information needed to target resources and build collaborative partnerships with outside stakeholders. The measurement system is embodied in the "Secretary's Quarterly Performance Report" (SQPR), which the FDEP distributes to all stakeholders via hard copy and the Internet. The FDEP's measurement system is different from traditional balanced scorecard measurement systems in that customer and employee satisfaction are not included in the measurement system.

The goal of the FDEP's measurement/management system is to identify environmental problems and the impacts that appear to be causing the greatest environmental harm as soon as possible so that roles for each stakeholder can be identified and implemented. Roles for regulatory agencies include such activities as addressing noncompliance and conducting research, while the roles for outside stakeholders include such activities as lowering energy usage and implementing best management practices.

The SQPR communicates the FDEP programs, its intensive performance measurement system activities, and its outcomes to its stakeholders.

Key Concepts

- The FDEP is building the capacity to conduct community-based environmental management.
- The FDEP has no threats—all are involved; databases and action plans are shared efforts.
- There is a process of involvement at all levels: individuals and local, state, and federal governments.

Key Points

- Flexibility through measurement, discretion through delegation, and trust through accountability
- Performance Partnership Agreement

- Joint Compliance and Enforcement Plan—a detailed plan to identify and address state/federal priorities
- Identify issues and best tools to resolve them: root cause analysis
- Accountability—through Secretary's Quarterly Performance Report
- Information
- Improvement—one-stop integrated database.

The future for the FDEP leads them toward working with stakeholders to identify Florida's environmental priorities, increasing department accountability, improving its performance measurement system, and streamlining reporting to the EPA.

Process for Establishing a Set of Measures

As noted previously, the FDEP's performance measurement system does not attempt to measure customer or employee satisfaction. However, the FDEP does have a set of performance measures that focus on the outcomes they are striving to achieve, such as healthy air and water, and that supply the contextual information needed to evaluate changes in the observed outcomes (see framework below). Their outcome measures are exemplary. The resource efficiency measures are evolving and are considered as critical to their overall success.

The seriousness of using a performance-based approach to their agency began when their secretary said, "Where do we put our resources, what are our outcomes, and what are we looking for?" The FDEP took the initiative and consulted with Malcolm Sparrow from Harvard University to develop the best way to approach performance planning.

This resulted in the following four-tier framework:

1. Environmental and public health outcome indicators. This is the most important tier and tracks the outcomes the department is working for: clean air and water, safe drinking water, healthy fish, and unspoiled Florida to enjoy.

2. Behavioral and cultural measures. These track the change we see in the way stakeholders behave toward the environment: the compliance rate of the various facilities, per-capita energy improving ecosystems, adoption of best management practices, common sense regulation efforts, etc.
3. Departmental outputs and activities. This covers what the staff does each day: the number of inspections, violations, penalties assessed, etc.
4. Resources efficiency. This is about financial accountability, including accounting of the tax dollars with which they are entrusted to provide the outcomes of environmental protection, usage, and volunteer hours spent. This tier is the least developed.

Due to the very short time in which the system was developed, the internal cultural change management component was under-addressed. The FDEP is moving from an activity- to outcome-based management system to protect the environment and public health, but the culture change is difficult. A major lesson learned from the FDEP experience was that cultural change management efforts need to begin concurrently or before the effort to develop new performance measures. Currently, the FDEP is using the information contained in the SQPR to manage for results and guide its result-based management decisions.

Accountability for a Balanced Set of Measures

The FDEP has several systems they are using to maintain accountability, but the main source document supporting its programs is the Secretary's Quarterly Performance Report, which reports on established measures.

Measuring Performance Data Collection and Reporting

The FDEP is continually improving their methods of measuring performance to get results in protecting public health and the environment. For example, with the generation of statistically valid compliance rates, the age-old enforcement question of "are enforcement numbers going up or down?" is supplemented with the much more relevant question "are compliance rates going up or down?" If compliance rates are increasing, then a decrease in enforcement numbers would be expected. However, if compliance rates are dropping as enforcement numbers drop, there is a problem. This is the power of an integrated measurement system.

When they suspect environmental or public health problems, the FDEP utilizes a highly structured process called Environmental Problem Solving (EPS) to identify clearly the important problems and fix them. The steps are to:

- Identify the potential problem
- Define the problem precisely
- Determine how to measure the impact
- Develop solutions
- Implement the plan with periodic monitoring and review
- Close the case.

A form of root cause analysis is an important part of the EPS. The FDEP identifies the factors having the largest impact on an identified problem and analyzes what can be done to lessen the impact of each factor. There are two levels of analysis: (1) analyzing trends and patterns of data to identify the factors having the largest impact on important problems; and (2) determining what is causing each identified factor so that the appropriate integrated response can be designed, such as enforcement, compliance assistance, and collaborative partnerships.

In developing compliance rates, the FDEP first decided to put a definition on compliance, that is, the distinction between "full compliance" and "significant compliance." Significant compliance is defined as the percentage of facilities with no violations that had an impact or the potential to have an impact on human health or the environment. Significant compliance is used to ensure that those facilities with violations that have the potential to affect human health or the environment are highlighted, prioritized, and dealt with in a timely fashion.

Another major decision in developing compliance rates was to reject the use of a "compliance status." It was proposed by some staff to use "the percentage of facilities in compliance at a particular point in time" as the equation to generate compliance rates. However, that equation would result in a compliance status and not a rate. Since the compliance rates were to be used in resource targeting decisions by comparing facility sector compliance, a statistically valid rate was needed. Accordingly, the FDEP developed a method for generating statistically valid rates that uses representative and consensus sampling to generate valid rates.

For larger populations, random sampling techniques can provide cost-effective estimates of compliance. By placing inspection resources into sampling modes, regulatory agencies can learn more about the location and nature of noncompliance problems within different sub-populations of the regulated community.

Analyzing and Reviewing Performance Data

The FDEP is rethinking its information systems to capture a great deal of data. For example, they can now store compliance and enforcement functions and track data based on facilities in lieu of the activity conducted. Several components to their data systems have enhanced the factors available to make informed decisions.

The FDEP also uses data from other sources to supply needed contextual information. For example, per capita energy usage data are obtained from the Public Service Commission, and Average Daily Vehicle Miles Traveled data are obtained from the Department of Transportation. These data points are critical to further understanding factors affecting the environment. For example, as citizens demand more energy and travel more miles in their automobiles, the amount of pollution emissions from power generation plants and from automobiles increases. Both of these increases in pollution may be in 100% compliance with environmental regulations and permits.

Each quarter, the data contained in the four tiers of information in the SQPR are analyzed and used to make management decisions by the identification of "good," "watch," and "focus" areas.

- "Good" areas are those in which an analysis of the tiered data indicates healthy or improving environmental conditions and high compliance rates. They are distinguished by such characteristics as good air or water quality in Tier 1, high on-site inspection or monitoring compliance rates in Tier 2, and an appropriate number of inspections to verify compliance in Tier 3.
- "Watch" areas are those in which the data show a moderate cause for concern. For example, the compliance rate for regulatory standards in a particular district may be lower than the statewide average, or compliance rates may be low in a district, but only minimal formal enforcement has been taken. Such situations suggest the presence of an emerging trend or pattern and require further investigation prior to taking specific action.
- "Focus" areas are those that need to be closely monitored due to concern about persistently low compliance rates or deteriorating environmental conditions. For example, if compliance rates are persistently low despite high enforcement, the agency may consider compliance assistance alternatives or implementing best management practices. In "focus" areas, it is essential that management has the flexibility and support to shift resources where they are most needed to resolve problems.

Reporting to Customers and Stakeholders

Once the "good," "watch," and "focus" areas have been identified, the FDEP issues press releases, which detail the department's findings. The press releases have significantly improved the FDEP's relationship with the media and environmental groups. In conjunction with the press releases, over 1,500 copies of the SQPR are printed and distributed to the general public as well as placed on the FDEP's Internet site, www.dep.state.fl.us/ospp/report/intro.htm.

Accountability

For improved accountability to stakeholders, the FDEP's data systems are working toward an integrated facility-based database system. Transparent accountability is part of their daily work.

The "accountability" factor is not popular and is being addressed via the cultural change management mentioned above. However, the FDEP has the strong support of the secretary and the deputy secretary. The "good," "watch," and "focus" areas mentioned above tie performance measurement to strategic planning because resources are redirected to address problems identified by "watch" and "focus" areas.

Benchmarking

The FDEP began its performance measurement work prior to most other environmental agencies and is viewed as the leader in performance measurement for environmental agencies. As such, they have conducted very little benchmarking. The FDEP has worked closely with the Environmental Protection Agency's Office of Enforcement and Compliance Assurance during the development of its National Performance Measurement Strategy.

Lessons Learned

The FDEP believes that the best method for developing performance measures is to focus on the results that you are striving to achieve (for them it is the protection of the environment and public health), then identify the contextual information needed to analyze changes in the observed results. As the information is collected, it is vital that it be analyzed, used to make resource targeting decisions, and distributed to stakeholders.

For further information, please contact Darryl S. Boudreau, Program Administrator, Strategic Projects and Planning, Florida Department of Environmental Protection, at boudreau_d@epic9.dep.state.fl.us. The department's website is www.dep.state.fl.us/ospp/.

CHAPTER 7

Making It All Work: Building a Strategic Framework

- Linking Your Plan to Day-to-Day Operations
- Linking Your Plan to the Business Plan
- Linking Your Plan to the Data Systems
- Linking Your Plan to the Budget
- Creating a Strategic Management Framework

> You've got to think about "big things" while doing small things, so that all the small things go in the right direction.
> —Alvin Toffler

Creating a balanced set of performance measures cannot be done in a vacuum. To be successful, you must involve *every* activity of your operations. Not only do you need to balance* customer, stakeholder, and employee interests, establish accountability, and determine the best means to collect and use data, but you need to make these concepts work where "the rubber hits the road."

Translating a set of measures into achievement of organizational mission means connecting those activities being measured to the organization's daily operations. While this is widely recognized in theory, practical application in the public sector has met with widely varied levels of success.

In Kaplan and Norton's balanced scorecard, the scorecard quadrants are linked with arrows representing the power and synergy of management action, that is, creating integration between the measures, action plans, and accompanying management action. Whether in the public sector GPRA

---

*REMEMBER: it will never be in equal thirds but should take each aspect into account.

framework or the private sector strategic management framework, that integration is what allows managers to monitor cause-and-effect relationships and design proactive strategies.

Those public sector organizations that have been through at least two strategic planning cycles know from first-hand experience the importance of institutionalizing, and then integrating, processes. The key to driving actions and results is to connect all the critical elements, namely:

- Connect to employees and customers
- Connect to the business plan
- Integrate with data systems
- Integrate with the budget process.

> The state of Iowa, in discussing lessons learned, said that to be effective the performance management system must be part of the daily activities of managers throughout the organization. It cannot be the property of a particular staff member, strata, or programmatic subset in the organization.

LINKING YOUR PLAN TO DAY-TO-DAY OPERATIONS

> The U.S. Postal Service has integrated the needs of both internal and external customers into everything the agency does. Its strategic partnership approach with customers has allowed USPS to become part of each customer's "value chain" by serving as both a supplier and contractor in the customer's day-to-day operations. For example, by working with their large corporate partners, USPS team workers could determine specific mailing needs, including schedules for shipping, marketing trends, and size of packages. Pre-addressed packages not only made shipping easier for the customer but also made handling quicker and simpler for USPS. Imagine being able to achieve both customer *and* employee satisfaction with one simple change!

Connecting to your customers and employees is vital to the success of any performance planning, measurement, or management and is a driving concept within the balanced scorecard. If you try to manage the performance of your organization in a vacuum, that is, not seeking customer and employee input, you may succeed in the short term but are definitely doomed to failure in the long term.

Involving your employee in the planning process makes him or her a part of the team. Moreover, communication translates to respect for the individual employee, an especially important consideration to public sector employees, who are dedicated to their jobs and believe very firmly in the services they offer. They know what they need to get the job done right. Just ask them.

> In Coral Springs, Florida, each employee develops personal objectives that relate to the city's key intended outcomes, thus connecting their daily responsibilities to the city's strategic priorities. Employee reviews include feedback from customers and supervisors, while supervisor reviews include surveys of their employees. This view of each individual as a member of the overall cycle promotes a team attitude. By linking to strategic priorities through outcomes, strategic goals, and the development of departmental initiatives, resources can be targeted and efforts more easily focused toward results.

Working over a long period of time with working groups and commissions, state and local governments have connected with their customers and stakeholders to a much greater extent than has the federal sector. The latter have, however, made significant improvements in this area within the last two years.

For most public sector organizations, linking to customers and employees is the greatest challenge. Turning an entire organization into a seamless team involves culture change all the way from the head of the organization to the individual employee and customer. It takes communication and leadership. Best practices that link the employee and customer to the various phases of performance planning and management are described in detail in earlier chapters.

LINKING YOUR PLAN TO THE BUSINESS PLAN

If an organization develops its business plan separately from its strategic plan or annual performance plan, managers and frontline workers alike will not know which set of performance measures actually "count," that is, they won't know what they're supposed to be doing or what they're trying to accomplish, any more than will the organization as a whole. Business plans define the day-to-day outputs, inputs, and processes that make the organization function; these must be linked to the overall organizational mission and goals.

Best practices in this regard include the following:
- The Veterans Benefits Administration has integrated its balanced scorecard with its use of business plans. Each VBA business line links its initiatives to its resource request in the business plan; the plan in turn links to the strategic goals contained on the scorecard. Finally, each strategic goal is then linked to the VA's strategic plan.
- The Coral Springs, Florida, business plan has several key components: an environmental scan, gleaned from input developed for the strategic planning workshop; departmental initiatives to put the plan's six priorities into action; a financial plan; and a system of measurement. This last includes the city's key intended outcomes and the composite index from which the Coral Springs "stock price" is derived. The strategic priorities and key intended outcomes drive the development of both the city's business plan and its departmental budgets.
- In its most recent improvement cycle, Austin, Texas, has initiated a business planning process to provide better alignment with its four strategic priorities. Each city department is required to develop business plans outlining its objectives and strategy for achieving the city's goals; resources are allocated using the completed and approved business plans. But integration of goals and achievements doesn't stop there. Individual employee evaluations are also aligned to the city's goals via "alignment worksheets." The planning process also lets employees help determine new performance measures to be used.

- The Department of Housing and Urban Development established a business and operating plan (BOP) process that allows for a continuous flow of information between headquarters and field offices. BOP development begins with the stated objectives in the departmental strategic plan. The process then incorporates the measures developed as part of the annual performance plan and departmental budget. That document, reflecting all HUD-wide goals and objectives, is sent to the program offices, including those in the field, which then develop their individual business plans based on the BOP. The reporting system has separate columns for the field office goals and the goal as stated in the annual performance plan. Headquarters offices report on the national level regarding the APP goals. Field offices, in reporting monthly on their performance, can see where and how that performance affects the departmental goals and objectives. When field performance information is collated into a report for the secretary, it reflects progress toward departmental goals and objectives as well as the achievements of the field offices. This dual reporting system allows those involved in departmental performance reporting to "double check" the national system numbers with the field numbers. This process is in its third year, and there has been a significant increase in involvement by the field offices in the departmental planning process and improved accountability at all levels within HUD.

LINKING YOUR PLAN TO THE DATA SYSTEMS

The importance of having a minimal number of systems is a matter of efficiency as well as one of control and accountability.

The state of Texas believes that the purpose of performance measurement is to provide information for decision making. It accomplishes this through an automated and integrated accounting, budgeting, and performance measurement system. Agencies enter information online, and measures are reported and updated on the system quarterly. The system thus enables strategic planning processes to be institutionalized and interconnected; the agencies use the resulting data to plan, allocate dollars, and manage day-to-day operations. Measurement data are used in strategic planning, annual agency performance plans, resource allocations, and other major policy and operational decisions. The integrated system is thus a vital element of the state's strategic framework.

At the Bureau of Land Management, an integrated intranet-based management information system houses all performance, budget, financial, activity-based costing, and customer research data to drive accountability and link organizational goals and performance measures. The MIS is available to all employees and managers via the intranet. The BLM's director recently established a "dashboard" of important performance measures that are tracked quarterly for progress and problem resolution based on the agency's strategic goal areas and robust data elements.

LINKING YOUR PLAN TO THE BUDGET PROCESS

Resources must be allocated on the basis of performance measurement and management. Otherwise, when a choice must be made between doing what is requested in a plan and doing what is needed to keep or obtain funding, the plan will always lose. Your budget must thus be inextricably linked to performance measures.

Virginia has been implementing a fully integrated performance management strategy since the early 1990s. The state's performance budgeting process represents a major evolution in the state's past efforts in strategic planning and performance measurement by fully integrating them with agency and program budgeting. By integrating these three elements into a single process, Virginia has been able to link agency mission, program priorities, anticipated results, strategies for achieving results, and budgeting.

In *Performance Budgeting: Initial Experiences Under the Results Act in Linking Plans With Budget Experiences*, General Accounting Office auditors reviewed 35 agencies' FY 1999 performance plans to determine how well their spending decisions were tied to their performance goals, as required under the Results Act. The agencies with the best practices had performance plans that clarified how resources relate to results and had two things in common. First, these agencies used simple links between activities and goals. Second, they integrated budget justifications with performance plans.

Virginia's performance budgeting process fully integrates strategic planning and performance measurement with agency and program budgeting—and represents a major evolution in the state's decade of efforts in this arena. By integrating these three elements into a single process, Virginia has been able to link agency mission, program priorities, anticipated results, strategies for achieving results, and budgeting. The state's performance budgeting process begins with a comprehensive strategic assessment in which each state agency analyzes its state and federal mandates; customers and customer service; agency mission and activities; organizational strengths, weaknesses, threats, and opportunities; and the critical issues it faces. Based on these analyses, each agency then develops strategies, goals, and objectives that constitute its strategic plan.

> In the "deploy" phase of performance management at the U.S. Postal Service, the voice goals, performance goals, and indicators are communicated throughout the organization. Programs and activities are aligned with the strategic direction, and performance targets are agreed upon. Resource allocation decisions are made based upon the performance targets.

Agencies must provide information on three levels of performance measures, thus making performance information a vital factor in justifying budget requests and in executive and legislative branch funding decisions.

> The Natural Resources Canada performance measurement framework includes one set of goals, objectives, and draft performance indicators. The framework provides the foundation

for all departmental planning and reporting documents. It addresses reporting and performance requirements of the department's sustainable development strategy, federal science and technology strategy, and internal management practices. The department is currently allocating its financial resources according to the goals contained in the framework and has received special authorization from Parliament to align its budget requests to its strategic goal areas. These strategic goals are cascaded to subordinate components to align budget request and operational plans.

The U.S. Postal Service initiated the "catch ball practice," referring to the fact that, in performance management, someone is always focused on achievement of a particular goal, i.e, the ball is never dropped. For USPS, there is a level of performance expectation for each business unit; in its turn, each business unit responds with a budget requirement. Through this iterative process, a budget is developed. The unit's performance measures that result from this planning process reflect the voices of the employees, customers, and business results. As a result, USPS creates a link between strategic planning and operational deployment of performance measures. This technique is a top-down and bottom-up internal negotiation and involves the entire organization in the process. Network Two of the Veterans Health Administration also uses the catch ball practice to involve its employees in continual refinement of its goal-sharing program.

CREATING A STRATEGIC MANAGEMENT FRAMEWORK

If employees, customers, data, budgets, and results are all connected, you are well on your way toward having in place a successful strategic management framework. Such a framework creates an organization where achievement of a stated mission is clearly communicated throughout the organization and where everyone works toward the same goals and objectives.

In Texas, motivation has been translated into a very mature process that integrates performance measures into the decision-making process. The basic components of the system were developed concurrently in the early 1990s into a complete, interconnected system resulting in a comprehensive system of strategic planning, performance measurement, performance-based budgeting, and performance reporting, monitoring, assessment, and auditing. Though the system is considered mature, given the extended time in which it has existed as a complete system, it continues to evolve. Interim reviews and evaluations conducted by the governor, legislature, and state auditor, as well as other efforts to build upon and refine the system (e.g., the addition of benchmarking, customer satisfaction assessment, management training, and activity-based costing components), contribute to this evolution.

The U.S. Coast Guard and the Department of Veterans Affairs provide excellent examples of strategic management frameworks in the federal sector. The Coast Guard's Family of Plans illustrates the agency's strategic planning and strategic management architecture and has been recognized by the General Accounting Office as a best practice in strategic linkage. The architecture supports and institutionalizes the agency's measurement framework. The family includes the Coast Guard 2020 vision statement, the agency's strategic outlook, the commandant's direction, and the strategic plan. The strategic plan guides and directs: (1) the agency performance plan and related annual budget request, (2) operational and support business plans, and (3) plans covering special areas, such as human resources and information technology. The field-produced regional strategic assessments provide input to the formulation of the strategic plan and directorate business plans.

The Veterans Administration's Strategic Plan, FY 1998–2003, is grounded in the notion of "One VA" that "delivers seamless service to veterans and their dependents." To this end, the department is restructuring the strategic planning and programs of its component elements (the Veterans

Health Administration, the VBA, and the National Cemetery Administration) to function as a unified whole. Using state-of-the-art planning techniques, the department is creating a strategic planning process that will build a strong and resilient strategic base for the future. Key components of that planning process include developing measures of program efficiency (unit cost), measures of program outcomes, information systems that ensure that management data are available for each measure, benchmark levels of performance, mechanisms to link performance measurement to the budget, and mechanisms to link organizational goals and performance with individual employee goals and performance.

Strategic Framework And Coordination

A strategic framework and coordinated strategic outcomes provide the framework for appropriately integrating the department's research, policy development, and evaluation activities around its overarching strategic themes, including linking these to the budget processes. It undertakes high-level analysis of emerging economic and social trends as a basis for developing and maintaining a future-oriented strategic policy framework to assist the department in achieving its key objectives. This includes policy development, research and analysis (that crosses branch boundaries), providing expert advice and consultancy services to branches, and developing strategically focused budgetary processes and co-ordination.

For a coordinated strategic framework, the key objectives and strategies include:

- Cooperatively developing and maintaining a strategic policy framework for the organization, in relation to the budget process, that reflects a systemic, behavioral, and cross-sector approach
- Working with other parts of the organization to develop policies that cross internal organizational boundaries (e.g., mutual obligations and simplification of processes)

- Refocusing research and evaluation activities across the organization (including through consultants and other externally funded organizations) to align them more closely to the overall strategic policy framework, in close consultation with other parts of the organization
- Ensuring a strong strategic focus to budget processes and proposals through extensive discussions, and developing better mechanisms for monitoring expenditure trends on programs
- Providing expertise and disseminating knowledge of broad social policy issues to relevant areas of the organization
- Developing close partnerships with internal and external stakeholders (across all strategic outcome groups, other departments, academic institutions, and the community sector) to foster shared understandings on strategic policy issues and assist the organization in achieving its objectives.

Thinking, as Well as Planning, Strategically

Most planners don't think strategically enough. They don't look far enough ahead or know how to read signs of what's coming. If they do, they don't think through the ramifications of their predictions and translate them into step-by-step procedures.

Studies by such organizations as GAO and NAPA have consistently shown that organizations that undertake strategic planning enjoy significant improvements in effectiveness, efficiency, and productivity when compared to organizations that do not.

If leadership cascades throughout the organization, and performance management becomes an integral part of day-to-day operations, manager motivation and morale should improve. Properly done, it can instill a sense of satisfaction by giving managers a role in the creation of their own destiny. Managers will know what is expected of them; and when it is achieved, it can bring a sense of accomplishment.

When done correctly, a balanced approach to performance management should:

- Create a workable road map for bottom-line results
- Make the most of time and limited resources
- Use a logical approach to unify the goals of the organization
- Improve the cost effectiveness of programs
- Help an organization to serve customers and clients better
- Clarify the roles of every employee within the organization
- Write accurate, clear, and justifiable budgets
- Make communication clearer up and down the organization.

Consider These Variables

When putting together a strategic plan, many factors must be considered. Managing the complex internal activities of an organization is only part of the challenge.

The external environment—competitors, suppliers, government agencies, and customers (whose often inexplicable preferences must be anticipated)—poses one set of challenges. The interests of stakeholders, including owners, shareholders, employees, and the community-at-large, also have to be taken into account. Economic conditions, social change, political priorities, and technological developments, too, must be considered.

Beware of the Limitations

Of course, no one management approach is flawless, and a balanced approach has its limitations. It is not the answer to all managerial problems. External forces may not react as planned. Factors such as changes in economic activity or a sudden change in political environment are uncertainties that can affect the outcome of any plan.

A significant amount of time and other costs may be required for effective planning. This makes it important to apply a cost-benefit gauge to the process. Also remember that formal strategic planning is not designed to get an organization out of a current, sudden crisis. It may, however, help to avoid a comparable future crisis.

Do It Right

Performance management and measurement is hard work. It requires imagination, analytical ability, creativity, and fortitude. The size and nature of your organization will dictate the formality of the planning process. A large organization with diversified operations requires a more formal process than a smaller organization whose operations are less complex.

Do not discount the potential benefits of an outside consultant. Someone knowledgeable in the strategic planning process yet capable of objectivity in observing your organization can be important. By providing expertise and a fresh perspective, an outside expert can help you organize the planning process and guide you through it as smoothly as possible.

One Approach: The Strategic Planning Engine

Michael G. Dolence[8] developed a concept called the Strategic Planning Engine (SPE), which links strategic decision making with organizational key performance indicators. The SPE is most commonly used by educational organizations and provides a framework for making very complex and politically sensitive decisions in both friendly as well as hostile and uncooperative environments. SPE can help an organization organize and use past information, including earlier planning and studies, and makes it unnecessary to "re-invent the wheel."

Although used predominantly in education, the SPE can help a complex organization make strategic decisions at all levels. It is a simple method to follow and use, so it works equally well for either small or large organizations. It provides a consistent framework that ties each of the levels together automatically while at the same time is effective at keeping diverse groups of decision makers focused on the most important elements of the organization's success.

The SPE can integrate activities already performed by the organization. Analysis and planning documents created as a result of an earlier management effort, such as Management By Objective, Zero-Based Budgeting, or Total Quality Management may have already identified and defined a set of key performance indicators. These key performance indicators can be used as the basis for the new planning documents and may be merged with budget initiatives or program evaluations. Any elements of these types used in the overall planning and strategy development of an organization can be used in an SPE.

The SPE is designed to help all participating decision makers explore and understand fully the relationships between the organization, the objectives it seeks to achieve, and the environment. It is a method to help keep the organization aligned with its environment. Alignment is guided by the results of a cross-impact analysis that illuminates the impact of external and internal environmental strengths, weaknesses, opportunities, and threats (SWOT) on the organization's ability to achieve its goals and objectives. Brainstorming focuses on generating ideas that address all issues identified through the SWOT analysis. (For more information on the SWOT analysis, see Chapter 3.)

Developing a Strategic Framework

The following steps are recommended for the development of a strategic framework that links together the mission, goals, and indicators with the concepts of customer/client satisfaction and employee involvement/empowerment:

1. Develop key performance indicators.
2. Perform an External Environmental Assessment.
3. Perform an Internal Environmental Assessment.

4. Perform a Strengths, Weaknesses, Opportunities, and Threats (SWOT) Analysis.
5. Conduct brainstorming.
6. Evaluate the potential impact of each idea on each strength, weakness, opportunity, and threat.
7. Formulate strategies, mission, goals, and objectives.
8. Conduct a cross-impact analysis to determine the impact of the proposed strategies, goals, and objectives on the organization's ability to achieve its key performance indicators.
9. Finalize and implement strategies, goals, and objectives.
10. Evaluate the actual impact of strategies, goals, and objectives on organizational key performance indicators.

Figure 7-1 presents a suggested strategic framework.

Workshops

In following these steps, some organizations find it helpful to conduct a workshop. A workshop should be at least one day in length, but not more than three days. Some of the roles that need to be filled for a workshop include:

- A keynote speaker (30 to 60 minutes) to walk everyone through the overall process, and set the tone
- A navigator/architect who can consult with the executive team, helping them to develop and implement a strategic planning framework
- An evaluator who can assess the effectiveness of the current strategic plan, as well as any processes
- A coach who can work with teams to develop and implement strategic planning across all levels of the organization
- A retreat facilitator who can design a strategic planning retreat and can serve as facilitator for any planning sessions.

Figure 7-1

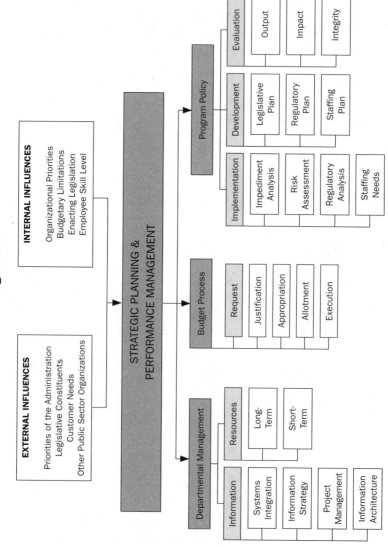

CASE STUDY #1: UNITED STATES COAST GUARD

"Semper Paratus"

Vision: *Ready today ... preparing for tomorrow*

Mission: *We protect the people, the environment, and the maritime security of the United States.*

Background:

- Approximate current employee strength: 35,000 military; 6,000 civilian; 7,600 reserve; 35,000 auxiliary
- Established in 1790, the Coast Guard has more than 200 years of history.
- The Coast Guard is an agency of the Department of Transportation, and one of the five Armed Services of the United States.
- Headquartered in Washington, D.C.; the Coast Guard is regionally configured with Atlantic and Pacific Areas, and further divided into Districts.
- The Coast Guard is a maritime service, performing its roles in three essential areas of responsibility: deepwater, coastal zone, and in-land waterways. (Deepwater is defined as the area greater than 50 nautical miles offshore.)
- Alone among U.S. Government agencies, the multi-mission Coast Guard simultaneously serves in *regulatory, law enforcement, oversight, emergency response, military, environmental, and humanitarian roles.*
- TQM concepts were incorporated by the Coast Guard in the late 1980s and have helped the Coast Guard evolve into an organization that manages for performance results using activity-based measures.

Business Results:

- **The Coast Guard was one of the first GPRA pilot projects**—and as such has worked with outcome goals since 1993, gathering and using data to manage toward accomplishment of those goals.

- The Coast Guard has developed strategic goals and corporate management strategies by which it manages its activities to maximize results.
- The Coast Guard has established a strategic goal for each of its major mission areas—**Safety, Mobility, Protection of Natural Resources, Maritime Security, and National Defense.**
- Coast Guard employs "logic models" to determine the optimal mix of resources in developing the best prevention and response strategies.
- Cost and value come together in a program logic model or value chain. The Coast Guard's strategic management process relies upon a model of internal processes (targeted by management goals), leading to activities (reflected by performance goals), leading to outcomes. In this model, the Coast Guard's performance outcomes are largely impacted by where the Coast Guard decides to intervene in a problem, by its particular strategies and activities, and by its internal management goals. The Coast Guard's selection of performance goals is based upon the logic model and causal factors. For example, Coast Guard targets are based on historical performance, trend analysis, and improvements currently underway. Some have been based on a defined performance level, such as achieving an absolute readiness index score required by the Department of Defense.
- Key to the logic model approach is the recognition that the Coast Guard is working in an interagency or "crosscutting" environment; other agencies play important roles in the logic, or causality models. In many cases, states and localities are part of the process. The challenge is to develop both a national strategy and local tactics—all of which incorporate best practices. Working with other agencies also helps those organizations leverage resources by combining project efforts.

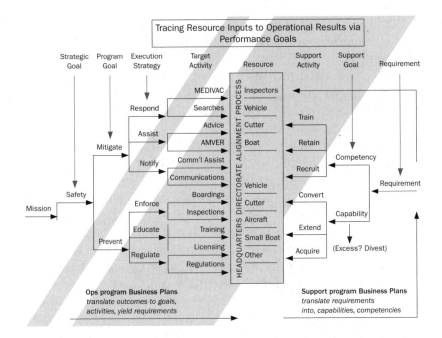

- The Coast Guard systematically evaluates where it fits in these cross-cutting program logic models and the appropriate level of agency outputs or outcomes. For example, NOAA determines fishing regions in order to protect fish habitats, an outcome. However, the Coast Guard produces an important output—patrolling ocean miles—that contributes to that NOAA outcome.
- Actual information is used to develop trend lines and set targets based on planned strategies. For example, the Coast Guard established as a target the reduction of the crewmember fatality rate on U.S. commercial vessels from the FY1998 statistical baseline of 43 fatalities per 100,000 workers to 40 in FY2000.
- The Coast Guard performs *Regional Strategic Assessments* (RSAs), in which operational commanders (Areas and Districts) examine risks, threats, opportunities, and de-

mand, as well as resource requirements to provide input to business plans, the strategic plan, and the five-year budget.

- The Coast Guard uses activity-based costing methodologies to identify direct and indirect costs in program areas and for developing standard rates for fully-loading costs to activity units.
- The Coast Guard will be conducting program evaluations to validate program logic models and their underlying assumptions and rationale.
- The Coast Guard *"Family of Plans"* illustrates the agency's strategic planning and strategic management architecture, and has been identified by the GAO as a best practice in strategic linkage. The architecture supports and institutionalizes the agency's measurement framework. The family includes the Coast Guard 2020 vision statement, the agency's strategic outlook, commandant's direction, and strategic plan. The strategic plan guides and directs (1) the agency performance plan and related annual budget request, (2) operational and logistics business plans, and (3) plans covering special areas such as human resources and information technology. The field-produced Regional Strategic Assessments provide input to the formulation of the strategic plan and directorate business plans.
- The Coast Guard has combined their Performance Report and Customer Service Report into a consolidated, corporate-style Coast Guard Annual Report. (Copy available upon request from Commandant, (G-CPP), 2100 2nd St. S.W. Washington, D.C. 20593.)
- In the Performance report, the Coast Guard includes for each of its performance goals a description of why it acts, key factors, strategies, coordination, analysis and evaluation (including a graphic of the target, information for the past several years, and the trend line), and key initiatives.

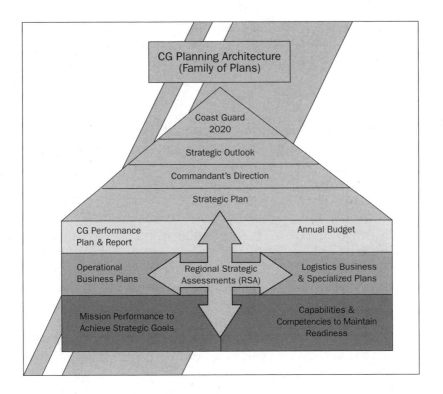

Customer:

- The Coast Guard had developed a strong customer service focus well before the advent of GPRA. This customer focus exists even in their regulatory role, where they stress the philosophy of partnering through the *Prevention through People* program. Constituents who are regulated are also asked to evaluate and identify problems, and to become partners in developing solutions. This has helped to reduce the number of inspections through self-evaluation, and in the development of risk management techniques.

- The Coast Guard has identified that the use of customer service standards and partnering relationships has a direct bearing on the agency's cost of doing business.

Budget and Financial:

- Budget considerations make it difficult to maintain a focus on outcomes, but the Coast Guard is developing a financial system to support performance goals. In terms of information management systems, with its multi-mission character, the Coast Guard may be the most complex agency in the federal government.
- The Coast Guard is implementing a five-year rolling budget model. With five-year budgets, which are updated annually, managers are encouraged to take a multi-year look, focussing on longer rather than nearer term goals, to realize efficiencies and economies to scale. The five-year approach also has the effect of dampening budgetary fluctuations; instead of quantum changes, budgets are changed only incrementally or decrementally.
- The Coast Guard has led the Department of Transportation in the development of an *Agency Capital Plan* (ACP) which links future capital investment requirements with outcome goals and develops the concept of return on investment for use in capital budgeting decisions. The ACP looks out up to 25 years from the current budget year.
- As an example of the Coast Guard's capital planning, the Integrated Deepwater Project departs from traditional acquisition methodology. The Deepwater Project is a performance-based acquisition to provide the capabilities for requirements identified in the deepwater area of responsibility, and has been designated a NPR Reinvention Lab.

Employees (Worklife/Learning and Growth):

- Recognizing that people are its most valuable asset, the Coast Guard has developed and supported Work-Life programs since 1992.
- Four years ago, the Coast Guard performed a comprehensive employee workforce cultural audit looking at organizational competencies.
- This month, the Coast Guard has kicked off a civilian needs assessment survey.

Benchmarking (Examples)

- The Coast Guard's aviation maintenance program managers have benchmarked with leading commercial entities to determine best practices and improve processes. This has led to their recognition by the Administration as an NPR Reinvention Lab.
- After benchmarking with private industry, the Coast Guard Yard in Baltimore, Maryland became the first marine construction and repair facility in the U.S. to meet ISO 9000 compliance standards.

Lessons Learned:

- MANAGEMENT MATTERS
- The importance of focusing on "results and outcomes."
- "Business Plans" are a snapshot in time.
- It's important to begin: "measure something!"
- When a measurement system has been established, begin looking at intermediate outputs and leading indicators.

GAO **Identifying Strategies for Prevention and Mitigation**
Coast Guard

Factors Adding Difficulty to Successful Response
- untimely distress notification
- incorrect or unknown information about distress
- poor communications with the mariner in distress
- severe weather at the distress location
- severe injuries which reduce the chance of survival

GAO **Identifying Strategies for Prevention and Mitigation**
Coast Guard

Prevent Distress
- conducting safety boardings
- CG Auxiliary safety exercises
- public service campaigns

Maximize Survival Chances
- continuous response capability
- VHF-FM distress network
- experts in search techniques and rescue procedures
- advanced search sensors and search planning models
- mariners carry effective equipment
- implement new technology in cooperation with international community

For further information, please contact either Michael Zack at mzack@comdt.uscg.mil or Lt. Cdr. Peter Troedsson at ptroedsson@comdt.uscg.mil. The Coast Guard's website is www.uscg.mil.

CASE STUDY #2: DEPARTMENT OF HOUSING AND URBAN DEVELOPMENT

Balancing Management Reform: The HUD 2020 Experience

When Andrew Cuomo took over as Secretary of Housing and Urban Development, he faced the challenge of restoring the reputation of a department. HUD's reputation was one of mismanagement at best and malfeasance at worst. Secretary Cuomo set out to change HUD and restore the public's trust in a department established to serve America's neediest populations.

To achieve this, he would need to accomplish a major transformation of the department's programs and management operations. His defining principles for this transformation were:

- No "givens"
- Distinct business lines with the core purpose of each organization within HUD
- Need to match workload with workforce and skill with service
- Measure and reward performance
- Create changes with most leverage
- Examine privatization opportunities
- Master and utilize new technologies.

Extensive consultations were held with customers and stakeholders at all levels. One of HUD's problems is that their product delivery is frequently through third parties (e.g., state and local governments or community groups). The way HUD delivers its services and the speed of its processing affect the "middle man's" capabilities.

Major dysfunctions were identified by "change agents" (employees/customers):

- Proliferation of boutique programs
- Organized by program rather than function
- Process rather than performance emphasis
- Mismatched workload and workforce
- Management information systems not integrated, accurate, reliable, or timely
- Organizational structure had ineffective relationships between HQ and field
- Workforce had confusing mandates
- Stewardship of public fund was not a priority.

As a result of this consultation effort, primary management reforms were set into motion:

- Reorganizing by function rather than program; consolidating or privatizing
- Modernizing/integrating HUD's outdated financial management systems
- Creating enforcement authority with one objective: restoring public trust
- Refocusing and retraining HUD's workforce to carry out the revitalized mission
- Establishing performance-based systems for HUD programs, operations, and employees
- Replacing HUD's top-down bureaucracy with a new, customer-friendly structure.

Keeping in mind the primary responsibility of the department, the HUD mission became twofold: (1) to empower people and communities, and (2) to restore the public trust.

The secretary set out its primary objectives based on HUD's business lines, and, having established these objectives, HUD set about to restructure itself to deliver services in a more efficient and effective manner. Six strategic objectives, based in the strategic planning process, were established:

- Fighting for fair housing
- Increasing affordable housing and home ownership
- Reducing homelessness
- Promoting jobs and economic opportunity
- Empowering people and communities
- Restoring public trust.

The department established a business and operating plan (BOP) that has allowed it to link the daily operations of HUD with the strategic goals and objectives stated in the departmental planning documents, including the strategic plan, the annual performance plan, and the budget submissions. The BOP is the prime directive for work planning and management in department.

The development process included review and examination of:

- HUD's mission
- HUD's customers
- Programs, products, and services
- Processes and links across major program operations and organizations.

The next steps that were taken include:

- Align strategic objectives with:
  - major management reforms
  - new organizations
  - operations
  - programs
  - services
- Develop quantitative goals at all levels of program delivery
- Develop a workload planning and customer service delivery approach.

A Final Word

Traditionally, most public sector organizations have measured their organizational performance by focusing on internal or process performance, looking at factors such as the number of positions allotted, number of programs controlled, or the size of the budget for the fiscal year. On the other hand, private sector businesses have focused on the financial measures of their bottom line: return on investment, market share, and earnings per share.

Alone, neither of these approaches provides the full perspective of an organization's performance that a manager needs to manage effectively. But by balancing internal and process measures with results and financial measures, managers find they have a more complete picture and know where to make improvements.

Robert Kaplan and David Norton introduced the "balanced scorecard" in the early 1990s. Measures established using this concept give managers a comprehensive view of the organization's performance and include both process and results measures. Kaplan and Norton compare the balanced scorecard to the dials and indicators in an airplane cockpit. For the complex task of flying an airplane, pilots need detailed information about fuel, air speed, altitude, bearing, and other indicators that summarize the current and predicted environment. Reliance on one instrument can be fatal. By the same token, the variety of problems that arise in the management of an organization requires managers to be able to view performance in several areas at the same time. A balanced scorecard or a balanced set of measures provides that valuable information.

The balanced scorecard is a management framework that turns business strategy into action by communicating strategic intent to the entire organization and motivating employees through measurement of key performance indicators. Thus, with a scorecard on the desktop, a manager can monitor business performance against established targets on all levels of the organization.

The philosophy behind the balanced scorecard is simple: set targets and measure the performance related to strategic and operational objectives. In developing these objectives and measures, work with those affected by the activities of your organization to determine what means the most to them. Involve employees. Talk to stakeholders and customers. As a public sector organization, keep in mind that there is a public governance responsibility to the taxpayer as well.

To do all of this correctly, the organization must develop a balanced picture of the organization, focusing on financial as well as non-financial, internal as well as external, and performance as well as outcome measures.

To implement a balanced approach successfully, you must:

- Obtain a commitment from organizational leadership and be sure that leadership cascades throughout the organization. If it focuses solely on the administration of a public sector organization, it will shift with elections and have no sustainability.
- Allow the organization to define strategic objectives and key performance indicators. Work with the employees. Public sector employees are dedicated individuals who know what they need to do their jobs correctly.
- Involve stakeholders, customers, and employees. Consultation—extensive and ongoing—is a must.
- Develop a communication plan. Communication is key to the process. Without it, the efforts of a public sector organization become isolated from those who are affected by its activities.

- Use technology to collect, analyze, and use performance information. Don't be afraid to spend the time and money to do it right; it will be worth it.

My hope is that this book will provide public sector managers with best practices and new ideas to try as we all find our way toward improved performance and accountability for the public sector.

Notes

For further information on the work of Drs. Kaplan and Norton, please refer to their website, www.bscol.com.

For further information on the work of Dr. Sveiby, please refer to his website, www.sveiby.com.

"The Balanced Scorecard for Public-Sector Organizations," Robert S. Kaplan, Balanced Scorecard Report (November-December 1999).

Special thanks to Sharon Caudle, Ph.D., of the GAO for her assistance with this section.

The definitions are, in part, from the Interstate Conference of Employment Security Agencies, a national organization of state administrators of unemployment insurance, employment and training services, and labor market information programs.

"The United States Postal Service: Customer Focused Change" by Sue Deagle. The Business of Government, Fall 1999. The Pricewaterhouse Coopers Endowment, Arlington, VA.

See endnote 3.

For more information on this concept, please refer to www.mgdolence.com.

APPENDIX

Balanced Measures Study Team Members

Audrey Borja
Food and Drug Administration (HHS)
Performance Results Staff, Office of Regulatory Affairs
Telephone: (301) 827-4225
Fax: (301) 827-0963
E-mail: Aborja@ora.fda.gov

Jerry Chatham
Department of Veterans Affairs
Telephone: (202) 273-5280
Fax: (202) 273-6629
E-mail: Jerry.Chatham@mail.va.gov

Stuart Haggard
Department of Veterans Affairs
Telephone: (202) 273-5053
Fax: (202) 273-5993
E-mail: Stuart.Haggard@mail.va.gov

Amy Hertz
Department of Veterans Affairs
Telephone: (202) 273-5283
Fax: (202) 273-6629
E-mail: Amy.Hertz@mail.va.gov

John Kamensky
National Partnership for Reinventing Government
Telephone: (202) 694-0009
Fax: (202) 694-0002
E-mail: John.kamensky@npr.gov

John Keith
Bureau of Land Management (Interior)
Oregon Field Officer
Telephone: (202) 452-5159
Fax: (202) 452-5171
E-mail: J55keith@ore.blm.gov

Margo Kiely
Fairfax County, Virginia
Director, Department of Systems Management for Human
    Services
Telephone: (703) 324-5638
Fax: (703) 324-7572
E-mail: margokiely@hotmail.com

Curt Marshall
Department of Veterans Affairs
Telephone: (202) 273-7522
Fax: (202) 273-5991
E-mail: curtis.marshall@mail.va.gov

Michael J. Novak
Internal Revenue Service (Treasury)
Telephone: (202) 622-6768
Fax: (202) 622-6767
E-mail: Michael.S.Novak@m1.irs.gov
Website: www.irs.ustreas.gov

Valerie Richardson
Associate Director
Center for Improving Government Performance
National Academy of Public Administration
800 N. Capitol St., NW
Suite 115
Washington, DC 20002
Telephone: (202) 682-4010
Fax: (202) 682-1119
E-mail: vrichardson@napawash.org

Steve Ruszycyzyk
Office of Management and Budget
NEOB
Telephone: (202) 395-7482
E-mail: sruszczy@omb.eop.gov

Gene Sheskin
U.S. Customs Office (Treasury)
Telephone: (202) 927-0276
Fax: (202) 927-0276
E-mail: gene.s.sheskin@customs.treas.gov

Ava Singleton
Financial Management Service (Treasury)
Telephone: (202) 874-8780
Fax: (202) 874-7275
E-mail: Ava.singleton@fms.sprint.com

Patti Stevens
Fairfax County, Virginia
Department of Systems Management for Human Services
Telephone: (703) 324-7132
E-mail: Pstevens@co.fairfax.va.us

Bob Stockman
National Weather Service (Commerce)
Telephone: (301) 713-0159
Fax: (301) 713-0161
E-mail: robert.stockman@noaa.gov

Patricia Sun
Federal Railroad Administration (DOT)
Telephone: (202) 493-6060
Fax: (202) 493-6068 (FRA)
E-mail: patricia.sun@fra.dot.gov

Chris Tirpak
Environmental Protection Agency
Telephone: (202) 260-7538
Fax: (202) 260-1096
E-mail: Tirpak.chris@epa.gov

Peter Troedsson (Lt. Commander)
U .S. Coast Guard (DOT)
Telephone: (202) 267-1124
Fax: (202) 267-4401
E-mail: Ptroedsson@comdt.uscg.mil

Michael Zack, U.S. Coast Guard (DOT)
Telephone: (202) 267-1137
Fax: (202) 267-4401
E-mail: Mzack@comdt.uscg.mil

RESOURCE CONTACTS

The following individuals are also recommended as contacts for their organizations. Some of their organizations are included as case studies in this book. However, all are recommended for their knowledge in the field of balancing measures and performance management. The federal agencies are listed together first, under the department (e.g., FAA is found under Transportation).

Agriculture

Animal Plant Health Inspection Service (USDA)
Eva Ring
Telephone: (301) 734-3582
E-mail: eva.p.ring@usda.gov

Food and Nutrition Service
Boyd Kowal
Telephone: (703) 305-2130
E-mail: boyd.kowal@fns.usda.gov

Food Safety and Inspection Service
A. Charles Danner
Telephone: (202) 501-7136
E-mail: charles.danner@dchqexs1.hqnet.usda.gov

Forest Service
Kathy Maloney
Telephone: (202) 205-1031
E-mail: kathy.maloney/wo@fs.us

Commerce

Patent and Trademark Office
Office of the Comptroller and Deputy Chief Financial
    Officer
Telephone: (703) 305-8161
Websites: www.uspto.gov/web/offices/com/corpplan/
    index.html
or
www.uspto.gov/web/offices/com/annual/index.html

Bureau of the Census
Joe Bellomo
Telephone: (301) 457-2327
E-mail: joseph.p.bellomo@ccmail.census.gov

National Weather Service
Bob Stockman, Strategic Planner
Telephone: (301) 713-0159
Fax: (301) 713-0161
E-mail: robert.stockman@noaa.gov

National Marine Fisheries
Jim Cohen
E-mail: jim.cohen@noaa.gov

Defense
William E. Mounts
Telephone: (703) 614-3882
E-mail: mountsw@acq.osd.mil

Education
Student Financial Services
Cyndi Reynolds
Telephone: (202) 708-9248
E-mail: cyndi_reynolds@ed.gov

Energy
Steve Logan
Telephone: (202) 586-9048
Website: www.pr.doe.gov/bsc001.htm

Environmental Protection Agency
Josh Baylson
Telephone: (202) 260-3644
E-mail: baylson.joshua@epa.gov

Federal Deposit Insurance Corporation
Gordon Goeke, Analyst
Telephone: (202) 416-4067
E-mail: Gogoeke@fdic.gov
Website: www.fdic.gov

Federal Trade Commission
Lenore Rodriquez
Telephone: (202) 326-2190
Fax: (202) 326-2329
E-mail: lrodriquez@ftc.gov
Website: www.ftc.gov

General Accounting Office, San Francisco
Sharon Caudle
Telephone: (415) 904-2280
E-mail: Caudles.sfro@gao.gov

General Services Administration
Rich Gudaitis
Telephone: (202) 501-1037
E-mail: rich.gudaitis@gsa.gov

Health and Human Services
Administration for Children and Families
Mary Ann MacKenzie
Telephone: (202) 401-5272
E-mail: ml@acf.dhhs.gov

Health Care Financing Administration
Elizabeth Richter
Director, Division of Financial Data Analysis
Telephone: (410) 786-7290
E-mail: LRichter@hcfa.gov

Food and Drug Administration
Paul Coppinger
Telephone: (301) 827-5292
E-mail: pcopping@test.oc.fda.gov

Housing and Urban Development
Betty Thompson
Office of Departmental Operations and Coordination
Telephone: (202) 708-2806
E-mail: Betty_Thompson@HUD.gov
Website: www.hud.gov

Interior
Bureau of Land Management
Carl Zulick
Management Systems Group
Telephone: (202) 452-5155
Website: www.blm.gov

National Park Service
Heather Huyck
Telephone: (303) 987-6770
E-mail: heather_huyck@nps.gov

Justice
Immigration and Naturalization Service
Paul Astrow
Telephone: (202) 305-4155
E-mail: paul.w.astrow@usdoj.gov

National Aeronautics and Space Administration
Headquarters
Judy Tenney
E-mail: Judy.tenney@hq.nasa.gov

Langley Research Center
Belinda Adams
Telephone: (757) 864-8990
E-mail: b.h.adams@larc.nasa.gov

Nuclear Regulatory Commission
Richard R. Rough
Director, Division of Planning, Budget, and Analysis
Telephone: (301) 415-7540
E-mail: RRR@nrc.gov
Website: www.nrc.gov

Occupational Safety and Health Administration
Paula White, Director of Federal State Operations
Telephone: (202) 693-2200
E-mail: paula.white@osha.no.osha.gov

Office of Personnel Management
Mary Strand
Telephone: (202) 606-1704
E-mail: mastrand@opm.gov

Postal Service
Patrick Mendonca
Telephone: (202) 268-6070
E-mail: pmendonca@email.usps.gov

Securities and Exchange Commission
Michael Erickson
Financial Management Analyst
Telephone: (202) 942-0347
E-mail: EricksonM@sec.gov
Website: www.sec.gov

Small Business Administration
James Van Wert
Telephone: (202) 205-7024
E-mail: james.vanwert@sba.gov

Social Security Administration
Carolyn Shearin-Jones
Director, Office of Strategic Management
Telephone: (410) 965-6210
or
Judy Cohen
Leader, Near-Term Planning, Office of Strategic
    Management
Telephone: (410) 965-2045
E-mail: judy.cohen@ssa.gov

State
Passport Services, Bureau of Consular Affairs
Liz Soyster
E-mail: Soystereb@state.gov

Transportation
Federal Aviation Administration Logistics Center
Rosalie Manley
Telephone: (202) 267-3009

Federal Railroad Administration
Alex Della Valle
Telephone: (202) 493-6210
E-mail: alex.della-valle@fra.dot.gov
Website: www.fra.dot.gov

U.S. Coast Guard
Peter Troedsson, Lt. Commander
Telephone: (202) 267-1124
E-mail: ptroedsson@comdt.uscg.mil
or
Michael Zack
Strategic Planning Analyst
Telephone: (202) 267-1137
E-mail: mzack@comdt.uscg.mil
Website: www.uscg.mil

Treasury
Internal Revenue Service
Michael J. Novak
Telephone: (202) 622-6768
Fax: (202) 622-6767
E-mail: Michael.S.Novak@m1.irs.gov
Website: www.irs.ustreas.gov

Customs Office
Harry Carnes
Telephone: (202) 927-0275
E-mail: harry.carnes@customs.treas.gov

U.S. and Foreign Commercial Service
Richard M. Irving
Telephone: (202) 482-3304
E-mail: d.irving@mail.doc.gov

Financial Management Service
Corvelli McDaniel
Telephone: (202) 874-7100
E-mail: corvelli.mcdaniel@fms.sprint.com

Veterans Administration
Veterans Benefits Administration
Dennis Thomas
Telephone: (202) 273-5442
E-mail: ormdthom@vba.va.gov

Veterans Health Administration
Tony Distasio
Telephone: (202) 273-8939
E-mail: anthony.distasio@mail.va.gov

VISN 2 (VHA)
Harry Ray
Telephone: (716) 862-6004
Website: www.va.gov/visns/visn02/vitalsigns.html

VISN 9, MidSouth Healthcare Network (VHA)
Janice Cobb, RN
Quality Management Officer
Telephone: (615) 340-2389
E-mail: Janice.Cobb@med.va.gov

Learning University, Minneapolis Campus
Kurt C. Gundacker, Trainer
Telephone: (612) 725-2160
Fax: (612) 725-2053
E-mail: GundackerKur@lrn.va.gov

STATE AND LOCAL

Austin, Texas
Charles Curry
City of Austin Budget Office
Telephone: (512) 499-2610
Fax: (512) 499-2617
E-mail: charles.curry@ci.austin.tx.us
Websites: www.ci.austin.tx.us/budget98/coacomi.htm or
www.ci.austin.tx.us/news/voice_survey.htm

Charlotte, North Carolina
Lisa Schumacher
Office of Budget
E-mail: bulbs@mail.charmeck.nc.us
Website: www.ci.charlotte.nc.us/cimanager/about1.htm

Coral Springs, Florida
Charles Schwabe
Office of the City Manager
E-mail: cs@ci.coral-springs.fl.us
or
Ellen Liston
Assistant City Manager
E-mail: egl@ci.coral-springs.fl.us
Website: www.ci.coral-springs.fl.us/CityHall/cm.htm

Fairfax County, Virginia
Margo Kiely, Director
Department of Systems Management for Human Services
Telephone: (703) 324-5638
E-mail: Mkiely@co.fairfax.va.us
or
Patti Stevens, Services Integration Manager,
Department of Systems Management for Human Services
Telephone: (703) 324-7132
E-mail: Pstevens@co.fairfax.va.us

Florida Department of Environmental Protection
Darryl S. Boudreau
Program Administrator, Strategic Projects and Planning
Telephone: (904) 921-9717
Fax: (904) 488-7093
E-mail: boudreau_d@epic9.dep.state.fl.us
Website: www.dep.state.fl.us/ospp

Indiana Human Resources Investment Council
Tim McGann
Telephone: (317) 233-0565
Fax: (317) 233-3091
E-mail: tmcgann@hric.state.in.us

Iowa
Mary Noss Reavely, Department of Management
Council for Human Investment
Telephone: (515) 281-5363
Fax: (515) 242-5897
E-mail: Mary.Reavely@idom.state.ia.us

Massachusetts Department of Environmental Resources
Carol Rowan West
Director, Office of Research and Standards
Telephone: (617) 292-5510
E-mail: Carol.Rowan.West@state.ma.us
Website: www.state.ma.us

Missouri Department of Natural Resources
Alice Gellar
Telephone: (573) 522-5530
E-mail: nrgella@mail.dnr.state.mo.us
Website: www.dnr.state.mo.us

New Mexico: Public Service Company of New Mexico
Janet Ruggles
Telephone: (505) 241-2594
E-mail: jruggle@mail.pnm.com

Phoenix, Arizona
Bob Wingenroth
City Auditor
E-mail: bwingenr@ci.phoenix.az.us
Website: www.ci.phoenix.az.us/CITYGOV

Texas
Ara Merjanian
Group Director for Planning and Development, Governor's
   Budget Office
Telephone: (512) 463-1744
E-mail: Amerjanian@governor.state.tx.us
Websites: www.governor.state.tx.us or www.lbb.state.tx.us
or www.sao.state.tx.us

Virginia
Herb Hill
Director of Strategic Planning, Research and Evaluation
Telephone: (804) 786-8813
Fax: (804) 786-4472
E-mail: Hhill@dpb.state.va.us
Website: www.state.va.us/dpb

OTHER

Atomic Energy of Canada, Ltd.
Mike Whitfield, Manager, Internal Audit
Telephone: (613) 584-8811
Fax: (613) 584-8040
E-mail: whitfieldm@aecl.ca

National Academy of Public Administration
Performance Measurement Consortium
Jake Barkdoll
Telephone: (301) 987-8596
E-mail: jakebarkdoll@msn.com

Natural Resources Canada
Mark Pearson
Strategic Planning & Coordination Branch
Telephone: (613) 996-6055
E-mail: mpearson@nrcan.gc.ca
Website: www.nrcan.gc.ca

Performance and Innovation Unit (UK)
Darren Welch
Telephone: 44-171-270-1514
Fax: 44-171-270-1568
E-mail: dwelch@cabinet-office.x.gsi.gov.uk

**St. Lawrence Seaway Management Corporation
(Canada)**
Carmen Nadeau
Performance Management Coordinator
Voicemail: (613) 932-5170, x3258
E-mail: cnadeau@seaway.ca

Service First Unit (UK)
Telephone: 44-171-270-6255
Fax: 44-171-270-5824
Website: www.servicefirst.gov.uk

Trademarks Office (Canada)
John Rombouts, Senior Advisor
Telephone: (819) 953-4746
Fax: (819) 997-1421
E-mail: rombouts.john@ic.gc.ca

Marv Weidner
Formerly with Iowa Department of Management;
now working with city of Austin, Texas,
on performance management issues
Telephone: (515) 282-4743
Fax: (515) 282-5933
E-mail: mweidner@cinetserv.com

Index

A

absolute readiness index score, 192
accountability, 40, 128
Accountability Report, Social Security Administration, 116
ACP. *See* Agency Capital Plan
acquisition, streamlining, 5
adaptation, importance of, 16
Agency Capital Plan (ACP), 196
alignment worksheets, 18
American Productivity & Quality Center, xi
Annual Accountability Report, 3
architect, leader as, 149–150
assessment, external/internal, 57–58
assumptions, avoiding, 110
AT&T, 135
Austin, Texas
  business plan, 178
  community scorecard, 102–103
  employees, 103–104
  overview, 22, 72–73

B

balance, importance of, 118, 149

Balanced Scorecard (BSC)
  history, 6
  implementation, 204–205
  Intangible Assets Monitor, compared to, 7–10
  perspectives, 8
  philosophy, 204
Baldridge assessments, 76, 146
Baldridge Award, 43
behaviors, desired, 129
benchmarking, 78
Benchmarking Code of Conduct, xi
Best Practices Symposia, 6
blame, placing on workforce, 115
BLM. *See* Bureau of Land Management
BOP. *See* business and operating plan
brainstorming, 68–69
Branstad, Governor Terry E., 34
Brooks Act, 5
BSC. *See* Balanced Scorecard
Bureau of Land Management (BLM)
  balanced scorecard, 39–40
  best practices, 42–43
  core purpose, 27
  customer surveys, 42
  focus groups, 21, 62
  goals, 41
  improvements, 41

management information
system, 94–95, 180
mission, 38
reinvention, 40–41
stakeholders, 25
strategic planning, 39
business and operating plan
(BOP), 17, 178–179

C

Canadian Parliament, 24
caretaker, leader as, 150–151
Cargill, 27
Caudle, Sharon, 121
CBO. *See* community-based
organization
CCFAC. *See* Consolidated
Community Funding
Advisory Committee
CFO Act. *See* Chief Financial
Officers Act of 1990, Public
Law 101-576
champions, 143
Charlotte, North Carolina
leadership, 145
lessons learned, 138
obstacles, 138
overview, 135
performance measurements,
137–138
priorities, 136
process, 136–137
scorecard, 139
chat rooms, gathering
information via, 119
Chief Financial Officers Act of
1990, Public Law 101-576
(CFO Act), 2–3
Chief Information Officer
(CIO), 5

client responsibilities, 14–16
clients, compared to
customers, 14, 29
Clinger-Cohen Act, 5
coaches, 189
Commissioner of the
Environment and
Sustainable Development,
Canada, 49
communication strategy
developing, 110
management style,
changing, 110–112
overview, 109–110
us *versus* them approach, 113
community-based organization
(CBO), 108
consensus, diverse audiences,
31
Consolidated Community
Funding Advisory
Committee (CCFAC), 107–
108
consultation, 28, 59, 61
Consumer Response Center,
FTC, 89
Consumer Sentinel database,
FTC, 89
conversations, types of, 120
Conversations with America
program, NPR, 119
Coral Springs, Florida
background, 43–44
business plan, 178
communication, 88
employees, 46, 177
Key Intended Outcomes, 19,
44
lessons learned, 47
performance measures,
22–24
Quality Fest, 46

Service Efforts and
Accomplishments (SEA), 45
strategic planning, 44–45
core purpose, 26
corporate survey, 128
Council on Human Investment
(CHI), 35–38
culture, 115
Cuomo, Andrew, 199
customer focus, 128
customer satisfaction, 40
customer service, 89, 114
customers
clients, compared to, 14, 29
compulsory, 33
leadership, 146
listening to, 88–90
stakeholders, compared to,
25, 30

D

data, how used, 114
decisions, management
functionally managed, 113
internally focused, 112
management-centered, 113
Department of Defense, 192
Department of Energy, 119
Department of Health and
Human Services, 27, 95
Department of Housing and
Urban Development (HUD)
business and operating plan,
201
dysfunction, 200
overview, 17, 179
reforms, 200
strategic objectives, 201
transformation principles,
199

Department of Transportation
Average Daily Vehicle Miles
Traveled, 171
core purpose, 27
overview, 62
Department of Veterans'
Affairs, 154, 183–184
Disney, 26
diversity, 31, 128
Dolence, Michael G., 187
Drucker, Peter, 93

E

educator, leader as, 148–149
EEO. *See* Equal Employment
Opportunity
85/15 Rule, 115
electronic conversations, 120
employees
consulting with, 29, 91
information technology, 94
involvement, 114
learning and growth, 40
responsibilities to, 14
skepticism, 92
surveys, 127–128
trust, 91
empowerment, 91, 114
EMSS. *See* Executive
Management Support
System
Environmental Protection
Agency (EPA), 30, 33, 173
Equal Employment
Opportunity (EEO), 128
ethics, 128
evaluators, 189
example, leading by, 149
Executive Management
Support System (EMSS), 133

Executive Order 12862:Setting
    Customer Service Standards,
    3–4
expectations
    accounting for, 19
    customer, 18

F

face-to-face conversations, 120
facilitators, 60, 62, 189
Fairfax County, Virginia, 11
    Board of Supervisors, 116
    budget, 106–107
    community capacity, 108
    Compensation Task Force,
        105
    Consolidated Community
        Funding Advisory
        Committee, 107–108
    Department of Systems
        Management for Human
        Services, 24
    Human Services Council, 17,
        116
    management indicators, 104
    performance, 105
FDEP. *See* Florida Department
    of Environmental Protection
Federal Express, 135
Federal Highway
    Administration, 61
Federal Managers Financial
    Integrity Act of 1982, Public
    Law 97-255 (FMFIA), 2
Federal Property and
    Administrative Services Act
    of 1949, 5
Federal Trade Commission
    (FTC), 89
feedback, employee, 151

financial benefits, producing, 30
financial management, 40
Florida Department of
    Environmental Protection
    (FDEP)
    accountability, 168–169, 173
    benchmarking, 173
    compliance, 170
    data collection, 169
    Environmental Problem
        Solving (EPS), 170
    focus areas, 172
    good areas, 172
    Joint Compliance and
        Enforcement Plan, 168
    key concepts, 167
    lessons learned, 173–174
    measures, 168–169
    overview, 115, 166
    performance data, 171
    Performance Partnership
        Agreement, 167
    reporting, 172–173
    root cause analysis, 170
    Secretary's Quarterly
        Performance Report, 167
    watch areas, 172
Florida Team Showcase, 46
FMFIA. *See* Federal Managers
    Financial Integrity Act of
    1982, Public Law 97-255
focus groups
    benefits, 64
    drawbacks, 64
    evaluation, 65–66
    facilitators, 62, 65
    meeting length, 63, 66
    overview, 32
    participation, 66
    politics, 65
Food and Drug Administration,
    33

foreign governments, xi
Forest Service, 27, 41

G

GAO. *See* General Accounting
Office
GASB. *See* Government
Accounting Standards Board
General Accounting Office
(GAO), 121
General Electric, 72
General Services
Administration, 5
GMRA. *See* Government
Management Reform Act of
1994, Public Law 103-356
goals, importance of, 57
Gore, Vice President Al, 151
Government Accounting
Standards Board (GASB), 58
Government Management
Reform Act of 1994, Public
Law 103-356 (GMRA), 3
Government Performance and
Results Act of 1993, Public
Law 103-62 (GPRA), 1, 3, 5,
155
Green Bay Packers, 72
Greenleaf, Robert, 150
gun violence, 32

H

Harvard Business Review, 121,
136
Health Care Financing
Administration (HCFA), 95
healthy land, 40
Herzlinger, Regina E., 121

Hewlett-Packard, 27
High Impact Agency Team, xi
historical knowledge, sharing,
117
history, strategic planning, 1–6
honesty, importance of, 121
HUD. *See* Department of
Housing and Urban
Development

I

IAM. *See* Intangible Assets
Monitor
IMCA. *See* International City/
County Management
Association
individual performance, 117
industrial espionage, 120
information technology (IT), 5,
94, 117
Information Technology
Management Reform Act of
1996, Public Law 104-106, 5
Ingraham, Patricia, 144
Intangible Assets Monitor
(IAM)
accounting theory, 8
Balanced Scorecard,
compared to, 7–10
history, 6
Internal Revenue Service (IRS)
accountability, 131–132
annual report, 133
balanced approach, 123
business results, 124
challenges, 122
communication, 130–131
customer satisfaction, 124
data, measurement, 132–133
employee satisfaction, 124

employee surveys, 127
fairness, 124
goals, 126
leadership, 153
measures, establishing, 125–126
National Treasury Employees Union (NTEU), 125
Office of Organizational Performance Management, 123
overview, 10–11, 33, 95
reviews, 133–134
stakeholders, 134–135
International City/County Management Association (IMCA), 6, 45
Internet
access to, 88
impact, 90
involvement, employee, 114
Iowa
budget, 35
Council on Human Investment (CHI), 17–18, 35–38
employees, 92
leadership, 37
lessons learned, 37–38, 176
organizational boundaries, 36
performance-based management process, 34
ISO 9000, 197
IT. *See* information technology

J

Juran, Joseph, 69

K

Kansas, 135
Kaplan, Robert, 6, 136, 203
Key Intended Outcome (KIO), 19
Kizer, Dr. Kenneth, 153

L

labor relations, 128
leadership
architect, 149–150
best practices, 145
caretaker, 150–151
communication, 146
educator, 148–149
importance of, 17, 143
responsibilities, 146
training, 144
legislative branch
consultations with, 90
leadership, 146

M

Management by Objective, 1, 188
management decisions
functionally managed, 113
internally focused, 112
management-centered, 113
Massachusetts Institute of Technology (MIT), 147
McDonnell-Douglas, 112
McTigue, Honorable Maurice, 144
measurement systems, 127–129

mission statement, 57, 60–61
MIT. *See* Massachusetts Institute of Technology
morale, 59
motivation, 59

N

Nadeau, Carmen, 162
National Cemetery Administration, 154, 184
National Commission on Restructuring the IRS, 10, 127
National Partnership for Reinventing Government (NPR)
  Conversations with America program, 119
  overview, xi
  Regulatory Agencies Team, 33
National Performance Review
  overview, 10
  reinvention lab, 197
  Treasury/IRS Customer Service Task Force, 127
National Rifle Association (NRA), 32
National Security Agency, 135
National Treasury Employees Union (NTEU), IRS, 125
Natural Resources Canada (NRCan)
  best practices, 51
  consultation, 49–50
  measurement framework, 90–91
  overview, 24, 47

strategic planning, 48–49, 181–182
vision statement, 48
navigators, 189
New York, 135
Norton, David, 6, 136, 203
NPR. *See* National Partnership for Reinventing Government
NRA. *See* National Rifle Association
NTEU. *See* National Treasury Employees Union

O

objectives, 58
Office of Management and Budget (OMB), 5, 25
Office of the Auditor General, Canada, 49
one-stop shopping, 41
operational responsibilities, 13
Organizational Performance Management Executive (OPME), 129, 131
organizational vision, 56
organizations, defining functions of, 53
outcomes, 58

P

Pareto, Alfredo, 69
partnerships, 17, 87
performance, levels of, 116–118
Performance Consortium, International City/County Management Association, 45

performance management
   principles
   accountability, 152
   establishing, 151
   excellence, 152
   timely action, 152–154
Performance Measurement
   Process Map, 53–54
Phoenix, Arizona
   communication, 89
   core values, 84
   history, 82–83
   leadership, 147, 150
   lessons learned, 85
   overview, 58
   performance measurement,
      83–84
   strategic planning, 83
Planned Managers' University,
   BLM, 41
POA. See Program for Objective
   Achievement
Presidential Memorandum for
   Heads of Executive
   Departments and
   Agencies:Improving
   Customer Service, 4
process improvement, 114
process mapping, 13, 30
productivity, 78
Program for Objective
   Achievement (POA), 93
public governance
   responsibilities, 11–13
public health, 34
Public Service Commission,
   171
public support, 89
public value, creating, 22–23

Q

quality, 128
quotas, 130

R

reengineering process, 114
Regional Strategic Assessment
   (RSA), 193
regulatory agencies
   common problems, 33
   customers versus clients, 32
Regulatory Agencies Team, 32,
   xi
reinventing government, 110
results, focusing on, 150
Results Act, 5
retreats, 67–68, 189
Revenue and Restructuring Act
   of 1998, 11, 127, 132
risk analysis, 132
road maps, 149
root cause analysis, 170
Rossotti, Charles, 153
RSA. See Regional Strategic
   Assessment

S

SDN. See service delivery
   network
Secretary's Quarterly
   Performance Report (SQPR),
   167
Senge, Peter, 147
servant leader, 150

service delivery network (SDN), 154

Service Efforts and Accomplishments (SEA), 58

Service First partnership, BLM, 41

Sloan School of Management, MIT, 147

SLSMC. *See* St. Lawrence Seaway Management Corporation

Social Security Administration
accountability, 98, 116
analysis, 100
best practices, 100–101
customers, 100
data collection, 99
goals, 97
key initiatives, 93
lessons learned, 101–102
measures, 96–97
overview, 30
performance reviews, 98–99
planning process, 97
Programs for Objective Achievements, 96
reporting, 99

SPE. *See* Strategic Planning Engine

special interest groups, 32

SQPR. *See* Secretary's Quarterly Performance Report

SSA Online, 116

St. Lawrence Seaway Management Corporation (SLSMC)
accountability, 162
benchmarking, 166
best practices, 165–166
customers, 164–165
goals, 160
indicators, 153, 161
leadership, 146
overview, 14, 160
performance, measuring, 163–164
pyramid, 163
resource allocation, 165
strategic plan, 165

stakeholders
consultation with, 11
customers, compared to, 25, 30
expectations, 29
leadership, 146
satisfying, 22

State and Local Government Team, xi

Sterling Award, 43

stovepipes, 113

strategic management framework
consultants, 187
coordination, 184–185
developing, 188–189
environment, 186
limitations, 186–187
overview, 182–184
thinking strategically, 185–186
workshops, 189

strategic planning
budget process, 180–182
business plan, 178–179
data systems, 179–180
day-to-day operations, 176–177
definition, 55

history, 1–6
phases, 12–13, 53–55
Strategic Planning Engine
  (SPE), 187–188
strategies, 56
Sunshine Laws, 45
supporting responsibilities, 14
surveys, 127–129
Sveiby, Karl, 6
SWOT (Strengths, Weaknesses,
  Opportunities, Threats)
  assessments
  definition, 69
  facilitators, 71
  process, 70–72
  strategic planning, 188

T

teams, 114
technology, 114
telephone conversations, 120
tension, 147–148
Texas
  best practices, 82
  future challenges, 81–82
  leadership, 81
  motivation, 183
  performance information,
    80–81
  state government, 31
  strategic planning, 79–80,
    179–180
Thompson, Joe, 155
Toffler, Alvin, 175
Total Quality Management
  (TQM), 1, 2, 58, 155, 188
town hall meetings, 118–120
traditional organizations, 112

training, 114, 128
Treasury/IRS Customer Service
  Task Force, 11
trust, 122, 128

U

unions, 95–96, 146
United States Coast Guard
  annual report, 122
  background, 191
  benchmarking, 197
  budget, 196
  business results, 191–194
  customers, 195–196
  employees, 197
  leadership, 146
  lessons learned, 197–199
  overview, 2, 30, 32
  strategic management
    framework, 183
United States Postal Service
  (USPS)
  accomplishments, 77
  accountability, 74
  analysis and review, 76–77
  best practices, 78
  catch ball practice, 182
  customer focus, 88, 176
  Customer Perfect
    management cycle, 74–76
  data collection, 76
  evaluation, 77
  history, 73–74
  leadership, 144
  lessons learned, 78–79
  overview, 19–20
  strategic planning, 78, 181
United Way, 108

V

value chain, public *versus* private sector, 25–26
Veterans Benefits Administration (VBA)
  benchmarking, 158
  best practices, 178
  BSC summits, 157
  communication, 159
  Data Management Office, 156–157
  evaluation, 156–157
  leadership, 144–145, 153
  lessons learned, 158–160
  overview, 93, 95
  performance, measuring, 156
  Reinvention Lab, 155
  resource allocation, 157–158
  responsibilities, 154
  strategic plan, 157–158
Veterans' Health Administration, 154
Vilsack, Governor Tom, 37
Virginia
  organizational alignment, 142
  overview, 122, 140
  performance budgeting process, 140
  strategic plans, 141, 180–181

vision
  importance of, 56
  leadership, 148
  translating into strategy, 150
vital view, 69
vouchers, 30

W

websites, gathering information via, 119
Welch, Jack, 72
Winograd, Morley, 151
Wisconsin, 135
work environment survey, 128
workshops, 67–68, 189
written conversations, 120

Y

Yucca Mountain Project (YMP), Department of Energy, 119

Z

Zero Based Budgeting, 1–2, 188